IT HAPPENED IN NEW BRUNSWICK

IT HAPPENED IN NEW BRUNSWICK

ALL NEW STORIES FROM DAVID GOSS

DAVID GOSS

NIMBUS
PUBLISHING

Nimbus Publishing Limited
PO Box 9166, Halifax, NS B3K 5M8
(902) 455-4286   www.nimbus.ns.ca

Printed and bound in Canada

Interior design: Kathy Kaulbach
Cover image: Claude Bouchard

Library and Archives Canada Cataloguing in Publication
    Goss, David
    It happened in New Brunswick :
    all new stories from David Goss / David Goss.
    ISBN 13: 978-1-55109-627-8
    ISBN 10: 1-55109-627-7

1. New Brunswick—History—Anecdotes. 2. New Brunswick—History—Miscellanea. 3. New Brunswick—Biography. I. Title.
FC2461.8.G66 2007   971.5'1   C2007-903977-4

NOVA SCOTIA
Tourism, Culture and Heritage

We acknowledge the financial support of the Government of Canada through the Book Publishing Industry Development Program (BPIDP) and the Canada Council, and of the Province of Nova Scotia through the Department of Tourism, Culture and Heritage for our publishing activities.

DEDICATED TO
Frances Cullen.
She always had a good
story for everyone who
visited her in Johnville.

Contents

Contents

Contents

We Worked Hard—We Played Hard

Introduction

The idea for this book occurred to me on a rainy afternoon on Grand Manan Island. I had gone there for a cycling adventure, but had been forced to retreat to the museum to read for a while to escape a deluge. The library has a beautiful room, overlooking Grand Harbour (when you can see it, that is—I knew it was out there that afternoon, but it wasn't visible). With no scenery to distract me, I spent some time looking through the books of photographs of the birds and flowers indigenous to the island. It took a while to get through the numerous volumes, but it was still raining hard when I finished, so I cast about for something else to read. That's when a book with the title *In New Brunswick We'll Find It*, caught my eye. The spine said it was written by Lowell Thomas; that didn't mean a thing to me at the time, but the title sure did. I knew it as a line from a poem I had used often when leading walking tours and bus trips, and which I had first heard from a member of the Saint John Fortnightly Club, G. Fred McIntyre, who had committed it to memory. I liked it so much, I learned it by heart, too:

Sweet Maiden of Passamaquoddy,
Shall we seek for communion of souls,
Where the deep Mississippi meanders,
Or the distant Saskatchewan rolls?
Ah no! In New Brunswick we'll find it,
A sweetly sequestered nook.
Where the smooth gliding Skoodawabskooksis
Unites with the Skoodawabskook.

Fred had told me a Saint John professor named James DeMille had written the piece in the late nineteenth century and that it contained the names of most of the rivers of the province. He could, and often did, go on to prove the point by reciting the whole five verses, but I'll refrain, as it is really only the first verse that is important to this story.

You see, when the New Brunswick Travel Bureau was first founded in 1927 to promote the province, they concentrated on fishermen and hunters, and the biggest annual event was the National Sportsman's Show held in New York each spring. By the mid-thirties, even though the depression was raging, tourism officials would go to the big city, put up a log cabin in the display area, bring along some live animals and a dozen guides, and spend a week or more sharing stories of the great fishing and gaming opportunities in the province.

It worked very well, as they got lots of press from New York writers and enticed many would-be "sports" (as they are called in New Brunswick) to come to the province. Sometime about 1935, one of those that dropped by the booth was Lowell Thomas, then a famed broadcaster, who had become known firstly as a result of interviews he did with Lawrence of Arabia, and went on from there to be one of the leading voices in radio in America.

As an offshoot of his travels, Thomas was producing a book a year on the areas he visited, and somehow he was convinced to do one on New Brunswick. It came out in 1938 and seemed to recount a trip he had made with photographer Rexford W. Barton. At least that's what it seemed like to me when I first saw it on Grand Manan, as its folksy nature and its many stories appeared to be the first-hand experiences of the author. I enjoyed what I read that afternoon and later got a copy from the University of New Brunswick, which I read cover to cover. It was at this point that I got the idea that I should do a similar book, perhaps retracing the steps Thomas had made, to see what remained and what had changed. So I began to gather stories as I travelled the province.

Advertisement of the first showing of the Lowell Thomas film in New Brunswick.

Then a curveball was thrown my way. During a visit to Carleton County, I mentioned my quest to Dave Steere of Presque Isle, Maine, who had procured a copy of the Thomas book, and was enjoying learning about New Brunswick through its stories.

"Dave," he said, in a phone conversation, "as much as I am enjoying the book, I don't think Lowell Thomas ever came to New Brunswick."

"What?" was my incredulous reply. "What would make you think that?"

As an American, recently moved to the area from Chicago, David knew a lot more about Thomas than I did, and he explained that the man had had a staff of researchers who did the background work; he didn't necessarily visit all the locations he wrote about.

"But," I protested, "this book is so intimate, so realistic, he must have been here."

"Not necessarily," Steere said. "You better check it out so you can say one way or the other, but my guess is he might have been there for one reason or another, but he did not come to write that book."

Later I learned that Thomas had eight researchers who worked with him in New York, producing one book a year, with more than fifty of them in fifty years, all to take advantage of Thomas's fame. But I still felt he must have been in the province to be able to write about it the way he did. The only thing to do was to prove it. As it turned out, that was not possible. This is what happened.

In a note of appreciation in the front of the book, Barton and Thomas thank a number of people for their help, and one jumped out at me: C. C. Avard, who had been the publisher of the *Sackville Tribune* and of the *Maritime Advocate* and *Busy East*. Ahh, I thought, his papers would have mentioned a visit by Lowell Thomas if it had happened. Looking through those papers, I found a number of interesting items.

The *Busy East* of May 1938 contained a review of the book. It didn't mention a visit by Thomas, but it did layout the background to the project, saying that Premier Allison Dysart, seeing that there had been books done on PEI and Nova Scotia but not New Brunswick, had made several trips to New York to correct that situation. If something was approved, I reasoned, then there must have been a contract and some record of payment. The public accounts of the province of New Brunswick for 1937 note a payment of $3,750 to "Lowell Thomas—On account of contract re production of Travelogue Pictures Book and Magazine article," but no more details are provided.

In the March 1938 edition of *Busy East* there appeared a photo of a group dining in the log cabin that was the feature display of New Brunswick at the New York sport show. In that photo C. C. Avard appears, along with D. W. Griffiths, director of the New Brunswick Travel Bureau, the photographer Rexford W. Barton and his wife, Lowell Thomas, and others. According to the caption, Mr. and Mrs. Barton had spent several weeks in New Brunswick the previous summer as the "personal representative of Lowell Thomas."

Further reading revealed that Barton had shot a New Brunswick film that summer, and that Lowell Thomas had provided the voice for that film. Avard's *Tribune* stated that the Lowell Thomas travelogue was shown in New York on June 2 and that comment from New York was favourable. (It actually played at Radio City Music Hall for two weeks; it was seen by an estimated six thousand people there and was expected to be seen by five million in theatres across the nation.) The paper also noted that "Lowell Thomas gave a fine narration." The *Tribune* reviewer went on to explain that the film was shown in Saint John on August 9, 1938, and that Rex Barton, "cameraman-adventurer friend of Thomas spent nearly two months touring New Brunswick last summer to make the film for the provincial government."

Ian Sclanders's "Man on the Street" column in the *Saint John Evening Times Globe* also reviewed the film, but not favourably. He criticized the film for its omissions and inaccuracies, opining that "Mr. Thomas muffed an opportunity to make one of the most interesting and most beautiful movie shorts of all time."

But back to the question at hand: did Lowell Thomas write his book from personal experience or from the experience gained when his partner, Barton, visited and shot the film? Though there seemed to be plenty of evidence that he did not visit the province, it was, as they might say in the courts, circumstantial. Proof positive, it seemed, would be to find mention of Thomas in the stories that were bound to have been carried in the papers of the province during the two months that the film was shot in 1937. But what two months? Since it could have been any time after the Victoria Day weekend, that's where I began. Day after day the papers contained no mention of Thomas or Barton arriving on the Boston boat on which the book claims they travelled.

After reading through almost two months of papers, a caption in the *Evening Times Globe* of July 17, 1937, caught my eye: "Filming of scenes in Province expected to occupy six weeks. Expected to reach 15,000,000 Theatregoers: will be supplemented later by book under co-authorship of Lowell Thomas and Rexford W. Barton."

In the main body of the story was the very thing I had been looking for: "Mr. Thomas had hoped to take personal supervision of the party who will operate in the province, but pressure of other business has made this impossible. It is expected, however, Mr. Thomas will visit New Brunswick at some time during the making of the travelogue."

Reading the papers for the remainder of that summer, it was possible to follow Barton's travels through the various reports: Grand Lake, Fredericton, St. Andrews, Grand Manan, Campobello, St. Stephen, Grand Falls, Edmunston, St. Leonard, Campbellton, Shippigan, Chatham, Sackville, Shediac, Moncton, and back to Saint John, after which there were a few more visits to places where the weather had not co-operated. Not one of the reports mentions Lowell Thomas.

I wish I was as clever as Lowell Thomas, but I am not. I assure you, dear reader, that I have visited every place you will encounter in the pages that follow. If I have even a bit of Thomas's skill, when you read the stories, you will say, "I wish I could have been there" or "I wish I could have met that person." And if I have a lot of his skill, and have done a really good job, you will go and see what I saw for yourself. In the meantime, I hope you enjoy these stories of New Brunswick past and present.

David Goss
July 23, 2007

They Made
New Brunswick
Proud

New Brunswick's Aviation Pioneers

As far back as I can recall, there has been only one airport in Saint John, the Turnbull Field in Loch Lomond, named after the Rothesay man who invented the variable pitch propeller and revolutionized air travel around the globe. This was in the twenties when airplanes still had pontoons and were such a novelty they were still called "air ships." They were a great attraction to the boys of Saint John who lived near the former airport, of which I know nothing and which was located at what is now the Millidgeville subdivision in the north end of the city, overlooking Kennebecasis Bay. As you will learn, some of the boys even came from far away, so that they too could have a first-hand look at the planes and the brave men who piloted them—and the brave women, too, as it turned out.

I've been lucky enough to meet two such men in the last couple of years, and they shared their stories with me. The first was Bill Giggey, who was born in 1920 and grew up in Millidgeville, and the second was Tim Ellis, a Rothesay boy, who took every chance he could to come into town and make his way to the airport in the early days of flying.

So, in the order I met them, here are their memories.

Bill began by telling me about the origins of the Millidgeville airport: "When I was seven, there was big talk about building an airport. What struck me at the time was the size of the equipment which moved in to build the airport. There was a big shovel that was steam driven, and they used to fire it up and dig at the surface of the ground. There is a lot of peat bog material which had to be removed as they could not find a solid footing. There was a lot of discussion of whether it was feasible, but they did go ahead and it took two or three years. This was during the Depression, and they had to find some work for the unemployed, so they used them to shovel and haul fill, stone, and gravel, to give solid ground support before they could build the runways. At the same time they started building the hangar, and before they had planes to put in it, they started a camp for the employees. They gave cigarettes to a couple hundred able-bodied men, who were paid twenty cents a day. They had the bunkhouse set up in the hangar, and they stayed there. With the cigarettes, food, and twenty cents a day, the men figured they were not too bad off. The turnover was quite high, however.

"After a time they had two surfaces built, runways, one going east to west, and the other going from south to north, in the form of an X. One of them was fairly long for planes of that time because they were flying the DeHaviland Moth planes that were lighter and not as fast as what we see today. The first plane that I recall coming in to that airport was flying from east to west, and it skimmed over the road where the St. Clement church is today. This plane came in and he was a student pilot doing his cross-country flight instructions, and he didn't count on the wind and drifted off the runway into the dirt and flipped the plane over. No one was hurt. He cursed and swore at the mud that he was in. That pilot, it was said, was Jimmy Wade. I know he was one of the first pilots to land at that airport, and later made his home in Millidgeville.

"The next accident was when Ruth Nichols came in. It was in the evening when the sun was setting, and she was coming in from

(left) Tim Ellis with his piloting certificate. (right) Bill Giggey with an old Millidgeville Airport certificate and a view of Millidgeville today.

south to north. At the intersection of the two runways, she was still airborne, and my brother-in-law and I were standing at the corner of the intersection as she flew by us. We figured the sun was in her eyes, and she didn't quite calculate the space she had left, and then she realized that she could not stop in time. She gunned it and thought that she could take off again, but she ran out of space and ran off the end of the runway over a rock pile and came to rest with the motor of the plane tucked underneath her seat. My brother-in-law started to snap a picture of her and she was fully exposed and was reaching for her purse, and she gave him the worst going-over. Swearing, and ordering us to 'get her out of there, get her out of there.' By then other people had arrived to help get her out. She spent a couple of days in the General Hospital, as she had hurt her back. She was alone in the plane, and was going to conquer the flight from west to east, from Canada to England, and was hoping to be the first lady to fly that route."

He continued, "The next person I remember was Amelia Earhart. She had Burt Bouncer, I think, with her, and they were aware of Ruth Nichols's crash. She had a successful landing in her Lockheed Vega, a beautiful plane and at the time, very fast. She flew over the continent, and she later lost her life over the Pacific."

The next recollection he had was of Jimmy Mollison flying from England to Canada. This was the first east-to-west flight across the Atlantic. With a laugh, Bill recalled that Mollison "flew across the Atlantic with no difficulty. However, he did miss the airport in Saint John and landed fifty kilometres away in Pennfield, in a blueberry patch. He later came to Saint John. I have a photo of me standing holding the strut of the wing as though I owned the plane."

Another incident he recalled involved a couple from north-western Europe, either Denmark or Norway, who had decided to fly from the Netherlands to western Canada. Looking to refuel at Millidgeville, they somehow managed to miss the airport and had to land forty kilometres away on the beach at New River. Bill recalled, "Once down, they asked if there was anyone who could help them fly to the airport, and this one young fellow from the Manawagonish Road area, Lancaster, said he knew the way and would help them out and he got in the plane and they flew to Millidgeville, where they made a successful landing. When the kid went to go out the door of the plane he stepped onto the wheel and went forward toward the propeller which was still turning a bit. The propeller hit the side of his head and shoulder and pushed him to the ground. They took him to the hospital, but he survived okay."

He also recalled a local stunt pilot named Scottie Sterling, who, he said, "liked to take chances. He was quite a ball player in the city, and he liked flying and taking chances." One of Sterling's favourite stunts was to fly over the river in the spring when rafts of logs were being towed down to the mill at Reversing Falls. "He would dive the aircraft at the boys on the raft and come so close they would dive overboard for safety," Bill recalled. In one of his most memorable stunts, Sterling flew his plane under the Reversing Falls bridge and out over the harbour. "He was reprimanded for this stunt," Bill said.

However, more stunts were to follow, with tragic consequences. Bill explained, "Later on, a Sunday evening, Scottie and a young fellow named Rud Brayley got killed trying a stunt. I remember the night. Dad was taking Mom and I to visit her sister in Grand Bay and we left the house and were at the corner of Millidge Avenue and Manor Sutton Road, and there was Rud all dressed up. So Pop stopped the car and said to him, 'Rud, going to town? Must have a heavy date tonight. I never see you all dressed up in a suit.' So we picked him up, but when we got to the airport, Rud said, 'Wow, what a crowd, that stupid Scottie is going to try an outside loop. Let me out to see what's going on.' So Rud left us. And he got involved in the stunt. Scottie had a special harness made so that he would not be thrown out of the plane during the outside loop. A lot of people were trying it, but he didn't have the power in the plane to take them over the top of the loop. We had our visit, and coming home along Millidge Avenue, the traffic was very fierce. Dad said, 'There's something has happened here.' We later discovered the plane had crashed on the back shore behind my father's store. Rud and Scottie Sterling were killed instantly. My sister was part of it, as she and her boyfriend were sitting near the very spot where the plane crashed. This was just before graduating. They were sitting on the rock and she was hitting him with an alder switch, teasing, and he wanted to take it away from her, and she got up to run away, and he ran after her. They stopped running, and froze, as the plane came down right where they had been sitting, and they were so close that the spars, from the frame of the all-wooden wing, and the splinters from the wood came out and cut her arm. She collapsed after seeing Scottie Sterling tumble out of the plane upon impact. We have a picture of her a couple days later, with her scar and wearing her graduation dress."

Newspaper accounts of the incident place the date at June 14, 1931. The details agree with Bill's recollection and even mention his sister's close shave with death as a result of the tragedy.

When I was reading Bill's story to Tim Ellis, he said, "I have always wanted to see a copy of that newspaper." I was glad to be able to share it with him, for he certainly had lots to share with me, which I now place before you to round out this chapter on New Brunswick's pioneering aviators.

I began my visit with Tim by asking him to tell me about his earliest flying experience and was surprised to learn that it occurred at New River beach, site of Bill's story about the European couple. The Ellis clan had a cottage in the area and that led to Tim's first opportunity to fly. As he explained it, "Tommy Carr lived in the North End of Saint John and he had his own little airplane that he had been barnstorming with up in Ontario. It had written in great letters along the side of it 'Western Ontario Airlines.' Plural." He paused for effect and then laughed. "It was just the one little Gypsy Moth plane with a baby blue fuselage and silver cloth-coloured wings. There were people like Tommy Carr who thought that you could make a living flying around the country picking people up for short fun flights for anywhere from two to five dollars per clip.

"Tommy got the idea from when he had come back from Ontario, and he came down New River beach and would land on the sand flats and hop any passengers that had the required money. Then, at the end of the day, he would taxi above the high water mark and leave the plane there overnight, as he would be flying again on Sunday. He wanted somebody to stand guard of the airplane overnight so my sister and I would take turns sleeping in the cockpit in case any strangers would come around with damage in mind. The next day Tommy would take us on a quick run across the sand flats, up over the water, around Haggerty's Cove, probably no more than about ten minutes, but it was enough. It was something that didn't happen very often in the province. This would be in the 1928, 1929 era. Tommy was one of the originals."

And that piqued Tim's interest in airplanes, which he continued at the Millidgeville airport, even though he lived twenty kilometres away in Rothesay. He started going into town with his friend, Pat Sclanders, and Pat's brother, Hugh, to watch ships coming and going from the waterfront. Occasionally, they would get to board the ship, thanks to Pat's father's influence as secretary of the Board of Trade. When the airport opened, the boys gave up ships for planes.

Recalling the excitement of those days, Tim told me about one especially memorable flight at an air show: "It was in October, and was cold as Greenland, and the three of us were standing there shivering. Then a chap sitting up in front of a Curtis-Robin airplane rolled a window down and wiggled his finger at us, so the three of us went over and crawled into the back area where there were two seats. I think the other two beat me to the draw and I had to sit on somebody's knobby knees. This was quite an airplane and it had a self-starter. Most airplanes had an arm-strong starter, meaning that you had to have strong arms to swing the propellor to get the thing started," he said with a chuckle.

"The Robin had a little compressed air on the motor, and you pressed a button and the compressed air turned the prop, and it would start on the first or second spin of the propeller. We took off and flew out over Saint John, and were very excited about the whole thing. The pilot was Captain Clifford Stacey Kent, and at that time whoever was in charge of the airplane was the captain. He was called 'Cappy Kent.' He was a very quiet fellow, and we got so that every time I was in for the weekend, we would head for the airport. We'd push the airplanes in and out of the hanger and clean them up and wash them down, run errands and do whatever had to be done. We just worshipped this Captain Kent. I don't know why he bothered with the three of us, we were always in his hair, but he did and he would give us a little flight at the end of the day, just a short flip around the field.

"Then there was a hassle between the flying club and another club called the Flying Sportsman's Arrow Club, and they got into legal problems and they were in court and Captain Kent said 'the hell with it' and went to St. Hubert's airport in Montreal and ran his flying service up there. He had been the club instructor in Saint John. He had his own little Gypsy Moth, he had acquired somehow, I don't know how; it was number 60."

What an amazing memory for details, I thought as he threw in the airplane number. I listened intently as he went on. "I was working in the bank and went up to Montreal for a holiday. I was born in Montreal and my relatives were all there, so whenever I could get away for a holiday I went there. I was staying with my uncle and aunt in Montreal West, and decided to go out to see Captain Kent. Right away he sat me in the airplane and away we went. At first I kept my feet on the rudders and after I got that mastered he let me take hold of the stick which you pulled back to go up, pushed forward to go down, and left and right. After a while, I think I had three or four lessons, then my holidays was up and I had to head home. I went out to the Saint John airport and got hold of Fred W. Hartwick for instructions. The cost was $10 an hour for instruction. So you could fly for fifteen minutes for $2.50. That's about all I would have every week to squander on flying."

He got his license in 1935 and still has the book showing all his practice flights. After getting his license, he had to put in twenty-five hours before he could take anybody up in the aircraft. He said, "I used to take all my friends whenever I'd go out. It was a wasted flight if I didn't take a club prospect out. A lot of these prospects were as poor as I was, and a lot of them didn't get into the flying game. I just loved it and I never got over the thrill of going across the field and into the air."

He had a couple of close calls over the years, including a miraculous landing at Millidgeville in the middle of a snowstorm. "I was pretty shaken. My mouth was dry," he told me.

On another occasion, he made two emergency landings at the Riverside golf course. Tim explained to me, "I was showing off for my girlfriend who really had no use for me, and I don't know why I bothered with her, but I loved her. I had flown out to Rothesay where we both lived and on the way out there was a thin layer of cloud and I was above it, so I decided I'd do a little beat up on her house, so I dove down through the clouds with the throttle closed, and when I opened it again to put the power on, there was nothing but clatter and backfire and black smoke coming back in my face, and I thought, my God, where am I going to go now? It was December, but the river had not frozen, and there was the number 2 fairway on the Riverside Golf Club. That was the only spot for miles around that you could have any kind of a chance to land. I made a swing out over the water and lined up with the fairway. I put the plane into a sideslip and aimed the tip of the wing at the alder bushes at the lower end of the fairway, and at the last minute kicked in the rudder and straightened the plane out. We set down on the snow on the runway and I was down. I thought, 'thank God!' Then to my surprise, the motor started up, and it sounded pretty good."

Surprised by his good luck, he decided to go back into the air. But as soon as he did, the same thing happened. And then—"bangity! bang! bang! Pow! Black smoke. God! Same thing again. So I swung around and back to the number 2 fairway again. The first time I didn't think that I'd make it; the second time I was sure I wouldn't."

But somehow he did make it. He didn't risk another take-off, though. Instead, he called an instructor at the airport to come get the plane. The instructor looked it over and concluded that the problem was ice in the carburetor.

These scares didn't stop Tim from flying, but after thirteen years in the air, he lost his licence because of vision problems. It was a sad day, he recalls. He had kept the licence for a lot longer than he should have through the good graces of a local doctor who didn't ask too many questions. "But by 1948," he said with sadness, "the doctor was gone, and knew I couldn't pass the vision [test], so I said, 'I suppose I can still fly as a student pilot who doesn't have a licence.' But the government officials said that I couldn't fly at all, so I gave my licence up."

He continued to fly from time to time, taking over the plane once it was airborne, and in fact, the day before our interview in February 2006, he had done just that at age eighty-nine. "Doing it that way suits me fine," he said. "Yesterday, we flew up around Darling's Island, toward Hampton, in toward the city. That cost me $104 for forty minutes. That's a hell of a lot more than $10 I used to pay for a whole hour!"

Lawrence White's Flu Medicine— Nothing Like It on the Market These Days!

If you mention the Village of McAdam to most New Brunswickers, they will think of the town in relation to its long association with passenger and freight trains. And while there are many stories with that connection that could have been included in this book, I knew from many visits to the village that there are other good tales, less familiar ones, that could be told about the area and its people.

However, it was not someone in McAdam, but David Haggerty of Haggerty's Cove who led me to the story that follows about druggist Lawrence M. White and the Chlor-Elix medication he developed and sold from his store on Front Street in McAdam. While on a visit to the Baptist church at Pocologan one Sunday, David came to me after the service, as he often does, with a package of historic materials he thought would prove interesting to me.

"By the way," he said as an afterthought when we were both getting in our cars, "next time you go to McAdam, try to find someone to tell you the story of Chlor-Elix. It was a wonder drug concocted by a pharmacist right in McAdam, and I wish it was still on the market. It sure perked you up."

That statement perked me up, and I couldn't let David get away until he told me some more. Others overhearing the conversation joined in to say, as David had, that "Dr. White's Flu Medicine" had saved many a life, and they too wished they still had it in their medicine cabinet when they contracted a cold or the flu. Some people remembered it as a golden liquid; others said it was clear as water. Some said it tasted like licorice, while others thought it had a lemon or orange flavour. Most everyone agreed that it was taken a spoonful at a time. A few thought it was more effective if followed by an aspirin tablet. A couple of people remembered that it was patented, and in fact David gave me a patent number, 16,900, which I was later to confirm when I had the chance to examine a four-ounce bottle of Chlor-Elix at the McAdam Pharmachoice on Harvey Road.

Chlor-Elix is one of a number of items that the current owners of the pharmacy, Keith and Valerie MacPherson, found in the drug store that Lawrence White opened and operated, and which they eventually bought, on Saunders Street in McAdam. Along with White's graduation certificate, his log books for use of narcotics and poisons, and a pharmacological book that gave him details about the drugs he could access, they display the Chlor-Elix from time to time in the modern store on Harvey Road on the outskirts of the village.

Old timers who see the display claim that there is nothing on the market today as good as Chlor-Elix.

The sample bottle is clearly marked as not for sale, and until I arrived there in July of 2006, it had not been opened since it had been sealed up, perhaps fifty years earlier. But Keith was curious to know what it smelled like, so he twisted off the top for a whiff. Neither Keith nor Valerie would hazard a guess as to what the contents might be. To me, it seemed like a product called Paragoric, which I recall my mother using when my youngest siblings were teething. White's book of narcotics lists the dispensing of paragoric from time to time, but his bottle of Chlor-Elix does not list this as an ingredient.

The entire label reads as follows:

CHLOR-ELIX

an effective preparation for the relief of

Colds—La Grippe, Asthma,

"False or spasmodic croup" and certain bronchial affections.

Trade Mark Registered White's Chlor-Elix

Safe—Prompt—Effective

Contains no habit forming drugs

Price 75 cents, 32 doses

Net contents four fluid ounces

DIRECTIONS

Adults—one or two teaspoons full every 2 to 3 hours

Children—8–10 years—one teaspoon full every 2 to 3 hours

Children—under 8 years—half a teaspoon full every 3 hours

No 16900 The Proprietary or Patent Medicine Act

Always shake the bottle

Manufactured by L. W. White, Druggist, McAdam, N.B.

Among the other items found in the store was an undated clipping in which White shared the story of his life as a druggist with a reporter, Thelma Ratigan. Unfortunately, he does not mention Chlor-Elix in the interview, but only says that the worst time in his career was during the flu epidemic of 1917, when "hundreds of people died and we couldn't do a thing to help them." According to the article, White took his training through the Saint John Pharmaceutical Society and served an eight-year apprenticeship in Fredericton at Burchill's Drug Store, receiving his diploma in 1910 and beginning his practice in McAdam in 1913.

Some folks say a doctor brought the mixture to McAdam after the war, while others say they have always believe it was invented by White himself. Almost everyone interviewed had heard that Chlor-Elix was first introduced during the flu epidemic as White's way of trying to help the afflicted.

One other piece of information gained from the MacPhersons was a contact number for the youngest of White's five daughters, who they thought might shed some light on the topic. Barbara Anderson now lives in Kitchener, Ontario, with her daughter Heidi Coburn, having moved there a few years ago for medical reasons. She was delighted to be asked to talk about her dad, and she has the most pleasant of memories of him. She confirmed some of the information from an article written about her dad in the *Woodstock Bugle* of September 8, 1966, as well as from her own memories.

"Dad was not a McAdam native," she said, "but was born at Robinson's Point, near Jemseg on the White's Cove Road. He began his apprenticeship with Burchill's Drug Store, now the Lower Ross Drug Store in Fredericton in 1902. That's where he met mom. After passing his pharmaceutical

Valerie MacPherson showing Chlor-Elix and other keepsakes from the era of pharmacist Lawrence White.

papers in 1910, he worked for a time in Fredericton and St. Stephen, also briefly in Calgary, Alberta. But anxious to strike out on his own, he came to McAdam in 1913 and opened his own drugstore. In 1925 he wrote and passed the state of Maine pharmaceutical exams."

Barbara worked in her dad's store as a youngster, and recalls one incident when there was a gas leak in a service station across the road. "It got into our well. Dad could have been really upset, but, as with most things, he took a lighter look. When people came into the store, after they got their prescriptions, he'd say with a chuckle, 'Need gas for your car, you can fill up here.'"

She recalled that he exchanged a photo of Queen Victoria with his brother-in-law in Montreal for years. Each year he would find another way to dress it up and send it and the brother-in-law would send it back the next year. "It was a running joke between the two of them," she recalled with a laugh.

But he wasn't a man to be crossed, she noted, in confirming a story a number of McAdam residents told of how her dad had been charged by a new RCMP officer in the village with having a nip in a public place, a remote picnic spot outside town where he and his buddies liked to go to relax. "Dad waited," she said, "knowing sooner or later the officer would come into the store to fill a prescription. And when it happened, he was told it could not be filled and he would have to drive into Fredericton. We laughed about that one for years."

Her father retired from his work as a pharmacist in 1955, but it did not last. After three years, he came back to work and remained in the field for another dozen years. In 1964 he was made an honorary member of the New Brunswick Pharmaceutical Association in recognition of his more than half a century in the field. Two years later he wrote up a history of the association's activities in York County to deliver at their annual meeting.

Commenting on the Chlor-Elix, Barbara said, "I don't know when he started to make it, but I do remember him making it up in the back room of the drug store. He kept it up to the mid-sixties, I think, when some government officials visited him, and when they saw how he did it, in a back room and a small batch at a time, they told him he could not continue to make and sell the Chlor-Elix unless he opened a laboratory. That's when he stopped."

She recalls Chlor-Elix came in four- and six-ounce bottles, but she lost the only bottle she had when she moved to Ontario. "I'd still use it if I had it," she laughed.

And from what I heard from the people of Pocologan and McAdam, I'm sure all of them would too.

David Russel Jack's Twin Legacies

David Russel Jack was a character among characters in Saint John in the late nineteenth century. He left behind two legacies, both of which are still extant and worth the time and trouble to look up.

Firstly, he was the publisher, and often the author, of an informative and highly literary series of books known as *Acadiensis*. Many of the articles contain information that would have been lost had Jack not taken the initiative to do this series. It's doubtful he made any money from the publications; in fact, he likely subsidized them from his more profitable day-to-day work in the insurance field. But writers and researchers ever since, including yours truly, have made money from what Jack preserved, as we have used his research as the leap-off point for projects of our own, or to check facts that we have come across, or to flesh out details in work that we have undertaken. Many researchers and historians since his time are indebted to Jack.

Many of the copies of the series are still extant, and they show up at used book sales with great regularity. They are quickly snapped up by those with an interest in the past. Some who buy them have, no doubt, been surprised to find in the copies rudimentary inserts promoting Jack's other legacy in the city, his cottage development at Duck Cove, which he called Sans Souci on the Bay and which consisted of twenty-three acres of property bought in 1890 for $1,050.

Several of the cottages still stand to this day, though all but one has changed so much that it would be impossible to recognize them as rustic cabins of yesteryear. However, that is not the case with one of them, which remains largely unchanged, and which allows you to feel like you have stepped back a hundred years. Although many modern comforts have been added, some of the contents and furnishings are just as they were when rich Boston families came to the cottage to escape the heat of the big city.

Let's take a look at this legacy, and at David Russel Jack himself, using the papers of the past to paint the picture. Jack was an indefatigable clipper of newspapers, and especially of stories in which he was mentioned. There were many, and he clipped both good and bad, as you will see. His clippings, beginning in 1898, are found in scrapbooks that have been microfilmed and are readable in their entirety at the Saint John Regional Library.

One piece, written on July 11, 1896, by E. S. Carter of *Progress*, a lively weekly that was published from 1901 to 1908, explains what Jack had in mind when developing Duck Cove. Carter wrote, "New Brunswick has many pretty summer resorts" and has "widely advertised her summer resorts," and as a result, "numerous visitors are

The only cottage left from David Russel Jack's development appears in this tattered photograph of a man and two children.

attracted from the United States and the Upper Provinces" in search of "rest, pleasure or novelty." He continued, noting, "Until this summer one of the prettiest of these places, Duck Cove, was simply a spot for private picnic parties, and daily the shore was thronged with those who sought to escape for a few hours the heat, confusion and rush of city life, and at the same time be within easy walking or riding distance of home."

Carter went on to describe the attractions of Duck Cove, of the possibility of visits to the historic Martello Tower, or, just offshore, Partridge Island with its lighthouse, quarantine station, and signal station, or the uninhabited Mahogony Island. Other possibilities included visits to the Smugglers' Cave at Sheldon's Bluff, with its full stock of guaranteed wild and weird legends, or the nearby "Pirate's Glen," which, he noted, "no doubt takes its name from some gruesome exploits of the famous Captain Kidd."

Of Duck Cove itself, Carter wrote: "Mr. D. R. Jack has built five pretty and comfortable seven roomed cottages at the 'Cove' this season...so that pleasure seekers of the day are not the only ones who enjoy its beautiful scenery and clear bracing sea air."

In a similar editorial later in the summer, he added information that the grounds had a dancing pavilion and an excellent tennis court, and from the tower windows of Sea View House, "a magnificent view of the surrounding countryside is obtained and one gets a glimpse of a picture not likely to be soon effaced from the memory." Sea View House was used as a location for entertainment in the evenings, and could be counted on for refreshments through the day including "tempting lunches and ice cream."

To reach the grounds, those arriving in the area by train could take the daily Shore Line Railway that ran past the site. Northenders could take a streetcar out Douglas Avenue, where the route ended because it could not cross the suspension bridge. Those from the central and southern parts of the city, and those who came from the suburbs as far off as Rothesay, could take the harbour ferry from Princess Street, then walk up a "charming road past the Martello tower," as one of the pieces described the very steep hill leading from west Saint John to the flats of Beaconsfield.

The clippings from 1898 reveal just how popular Jack's resort had become, describing outings by the Bicycle and Athletic Club, dances, and a Salvation Army concert attended by a crowd of thousands. For the 1899 season, Jack decided to expand. The *Daily Telegraph* of May 22, 1899, noted that "Mr. J. F. MacDonald has been awarded the contract for erecting the double cottage to be built by Mr. D. R. Jack at Duck Cove" and that a "log cabin for Mr. Jack's own use is being built, a new road through the property is being made and drainage work is being done."

In clippings from 1901, it is noted that Jack had nine cottages for rent and was building two more two-room cottages, "small, self contained with stove, furniture and utensils complete," to be "rented by the week at a small figure...as there is much demand for cottages of this class from Fredericton and other inland towns."

Another clipping from 1901 lists some of Duck Cove's guests, giving an impression of the prestigious clientele Jack attracted: Rev. Frank Hodgdon, rector of a wealthy congregation at Orange, New Jersey; Professor W. B. McVey, toxicologist of Cambridge, Massachusetts; and Rev. J. deSoyres of Saint John, rector of St. John's (Stone) church. A cottage adjacent to the Jack estate was occupied by Andrew George Blair, the minister of railways for Canada.

In 1902 an amusement hall was opened, and as a clipping from the *Globe* showed, it was done with a flourish: "a grand variety entertainment by the Empire Vaudeville company," including "Misses Barlow and Turner, the Ryan Bros., Charles Fay and Professor Burns...with songs given by Joseph Harris, Carl Ramsay and dances by William Roy. After the show there was dancing, the music being furnished by the Fairville orchestra." In that summer, too, the Canadian Pacific Railway began service to the area from the Carleton Station in the lower West side, with four trips per day stopping at Beatteay's Rocks, Bay Shore, and the Ferns, three other popular seaside bathing areas, before reaching Jack's Duck Cove.

During the years of development, Jack seems to have enjoyed vigorous health, for he not only managed to work on his dream resort, but to head up the tri-centenary celebration of the arrival of Champlain in 1904, and to offer public lectures on the various foreign trips he took. He was an alderman of Queen's Ward and worked diligently for the electrification of Saint John's streets, then under the grip of the gas company. He served as an officer of the Loyalist Society and of the New Brunswick Historical Society and was a member of the Saint John Fortnightly Club. He served as a member of the school board and as secretary of the board of the Free Public Library. He also took an active role in the life of the congregation of St. Andrew's church, and in fact wrote a history of the church.

He also seemed to enjoy writing. He first used his literary skills during Saint John's centennial, when he wrote an essay on the Loyalist background of the city and won first prize for his efforts. He continued to write features for national and international publications, university magazines in Toronto and Montreal, and brochures produced for the then just-formed Saint John Tourism Association. When he could manage to include a description of his resort in these pamphlets, he did so.

In 1903 Jack renamed his development "Sans Souci on the Bay," perhaps based on something he had seen on one of his trips to Europe and Asia. Taken literally, the name means a place without worry, and for the most part it seems to have been just that for Jack, though he did have some trying moments. Some laughed at his efforts and did not care for the highfalutin name of Sans Souci. Some people called it, derisively, "Jack's Enclosure."

He had some problems from time to time preserving the privacy of that enclosure. Probably the most interesting incident in that connection was reported, erroneously as it turned out, in the *Saint John Star* of July 30, 1907. It read:

There is a great deal of indignation among some of the residents of Duck Cove over the action of one of the principal property holders of that place.

The story is that a week ago last Sunday two little boys who live by the shore came down to a point below McLaren's Beach and went in swimming. They were within sight of some of the summer cottages, but were a long distance away from them and in fact were only noticed by a few of the residents. The property owner in question is said to have gone over to where the boys were swimming and to have taken their clothes. They remained in the water until they were pretty tired and then found their way to some of the cottages where ladies gave them wraps to wear home. It is stated that the boys were doing no harm and their presence was not objected to by other people. They were only ten or twelve years of age and had every right to swim at that shore.

Upon reading the story, Jack sent a registered letter to the editor of the *Star* pointing out how inaccurate the statement was and demanding a correction. None was printed, so a second letter was sent, addressed to the editor, H. V. McKinnon, on August 6. A partial retraction was printed, reading,

A few days ago, the Star *published a paragraph to the effect that a Duck Cove property owner had taken the clothing of a couple of boys who had gone swimming near the cove. The citizen referred to informs the Star that the boys had been warned not to trespass on the shore, that their presence was objectionable to the residents of this resort, and that they persisted in their plans even after being warned. He further says that he did not take their clothing as alleged.*

This did not satisfy Jack, so he wrote saying he would take legal action unless his objection was published. Receiving no reply and no further editorial consideration, Jack wired B. F. Pearson, the paper's owner in Halifax, requesting a meeting on the matter. Pearson was in Montreal, so Jack addressed a letter to him there, care of the Windsor Hotel, but it missed Pearson as he was travelling to Halifax via Boston. On August 20 Jack travelled to Halifax to meet with Pearson, only to discover he had left for Sydney, on Cape Breton

Island, and would then go to Moncton. Jack caught up with him there at the Brunswick Hotel, and laid out the story. A letter contained in his scrapbook gives his side of the story:

Neither myself nor any man at any time laid a finger upon either of them or their belongings. The whole episode was in full sight of a number of reliable witnesses whose evidence could be obtained were it necessary, the boys were not at any time in the water above their knees, they were not kept in the water by me or by any act of mine, the whole incident being over within ten minutes. Their clothes were not taken, they did not "remain in the water until they were pretty tired," the presence of men and boys bathing on this beach without bathing clothes has been seriously objected to by residents of my cottages.

And therein lay the crux of the matter—what we would call skinny-dipping today!

Jack demanded a complete retraction and insisted that legal action would follow if the matter was not dealt with as he wished.

On August 24 his chase around the Maritimes for justice seems to have paid off, for the *Star* carried this note:

In its issue of July 30, the Star *published, upon what was believed to be good authority a report of an incident alleged to have taken place at Duck Cove. The* Star *has since learned that the facts were not as represented and regrets that a statement so incorrect should have been published.*

After several more years of running his resort, Jack died on December 2, 1913, at Clifton Spring, New York, where he had gone in the company of his sister, possibly for treatment of a heart problem at the sanatorium there. He was just forty-eight.

His two surviving sisters did not share, it seems, his passion for Sans Souci, and it was broken into fifty-one parcels of land in 1924 under control of Duck Cove Realties Ltd. Today, a modern row of bungalows lines Seacliffe Drive to the east of the main cottage development and Cherry Tree Lane to the north. The properties between the cottages, in what is called "the Lollipop" on account of its shape, are filled in with homes, too.

However, there remain deed covenants that provide everyone living in the homes developed in the area rights of passage across lot seven at the embankment, so that they may reach the private beach Jack so jealously guarded. All also have rights to draw from common wells or springs (a moot point now) and to use of the common property, which includes the beach, the playground, and the tennis court, the later much improved and still used daily in the centre of the Lollipop development.

It seems, from the perspective of a hundred years, that Jack did the right thing in publishing *Acadiensis* and in developing Sans Souci on the Bay, for both remain to this day as his legacies, and should remain so for a long time to come.

Mabel Peters, Saint John's Playground Pioneer

In Susan Markham's study of the life of Saint Johner Mabel Peters, she describes her as the "mother of the playground movement" in Canada. Yet Peters has never received the recognition she should have for her pioneering work, which began in 1898 and lasted until her death in 1914, and which affected not only her hometown, but all of North America.

Saint Johners have been told for decades that their city had the first public playground in Canada and that it opened on July 3, 1906. As the hundredth anniversary of that date approached, the current leaders of the Saint John Leisure Services Department thought it a good idea to commemorate the event. They drafted the wording for a plaque that would declare Saint John's premier position in the establishment of playgrounds, and then they ran the idea by this writer—who promptly deflated their balloon by telling them Saint John was not first, but third.

However, I did encourage them in their quest to honour Mabel Peters, explaining that she was indeed the impetus behind the first and second playgrounds (established in Montreal and Toronto, respectively), and that the Saint John program never would have gotten underway without her determined effort to see it happen. And she had never been properly recognized for her role; in 1920 the local Council of Women had tried to have a playground named for Miss Peters in every city in Canada where there were at least two playgrounds, but their campaign was not successful. Not even in her home city.

David Goss dressed as A. M. Belding (left) with Jeremy Keats presenting flowers to Joan Pearce as the playground pioneer Mabel Peters (right) at Allison Grounds.

It was at that point that we decided to hold a couple of public events to correct the oversight of a century ago. So on Canada Day a Walk 'n' Talk was held in Fernhill Cemetery, where, dressed as A. M. Belding, editor of the Saint John Telegraph, who was such a great supporter of children that he became known as "Great Heart Belding," I led visitors to the gravesites of people who had helped Peters in bringing her dream to reality. Belding had given Peters space in his paper to tell her story, and his paper held a public campaign that resulted in the collection of $1,600 for the work. Buried near Peters was the mayor of the day, Edward Sears, who supported her cause, and near him, a gentleman who was deeply interested in playsites and playgrounds, Joseph Allison. So we visited all of them and told their stories. Finally, through the role-playing of local historian Joan Pearce, we met Mabel Peters herself as we gathered around her grave, and Joan related the basic facts of her life.

A couple of days later, we repeated the process with myself as A. M. Belding again leading walkers through the downtown, stopping at the site of his former paper, where we met with a character he had created to stir up the public, one Horace Hornbeam. We then passed the old city hall, where Terry Keleher brought Mayor Sears to life. Up the Princess Street hill we climbed to the site of the former Clifton House that Mabel Peters managed, where we met Lynn Adams playing the role of Mabel's neighbour and fellow local Council of Women member Alice Tilley. When we passed through King's Square, we paid honour to Joseph Allison, whose financial contributions got the Horticultural Association underway, which, in turn, got King's Square beautified. Before the establishment of the first playground, the four-acre square was one of only three patches of green in uptown Saint John where children could play. Mabel saw children in the streets, ducking among the horses, playing in dung-laced mud, or tossing balls in the old burial grounds, where the ancient stones might topple on them, or worse still, a member of one of the many active gangs of the era might lead them to a life of crime. It was not a healthy situation, and so she obtained the use of the Centennial School grounds, just a couple of hundred yards from the old burial ground, and there established the first Saint John playground. It was at that site that we concluded the walk, and where we met Joan Pearce, again playing the role of Mabel Peters. As "Mabel Peters," she consented to an interview from "A. M. Belding," and this is how it went, as if it were 1906.

BELDING: "Mabel, this has been a great summer for you. When the Richmond Street entrance to the Centennial School grounds opened on July 3, it was the first playground in Saint John and the fulfillment of your dream of several years. Did you expect the crowd that was there? I have heard there were three or four hundred children on the grounds through the day."

PETERS: "Oh, indeed, I expected it to be a busy day. There has been a great need for this program in this city for so long now, and especially in the area around Centennial School, where so many of the houses are built wall to wall, and big families are the norm, and there is really no place for the little ones to play except on the street. Oh, some can go up to the burial grounds, and enjoy a splash in the fountain, but only the older ones, of course, and there are gangs that hang out there. You probably covered the famous Doherty murder that occurred in back of Rockwood Park in 1902, and know that the burial grounds, and the area around the old Opera House was where they hung out. There's a chance any child going up there could fall into bad company. So, it's much better to have them come to a safe, fenced-in area where they can enjoy play and fresh air, and learn some new games, hear some music, and make friends."

BELDING: "Now, in my travels, I have not found it common for this sort of thing to be provided for children. Seems to me I read the idea began in Scotland, but how did it spread to Saint John?"

PETERS: "I really don't know how it got from Scotland, but I can say how it got to our city. I have a sister in Detroit, and my other sisters and I visit her from time to time. Clara, that's my sister in Detroit, is very involved in the playground program there. It was her idea that I try to get it going here in Saint John. So, as I am a member of the Council of Women, I suggested to them at one of our monthly meetings, that was back in June of 1900, that they should look into the idea and, of course, you know what happened: they appointed me as chair of a committee to do just that. So I started doing some background research, and I wrote a paper to be presented at the national meeting of the Council of Women in London, Ontario, in 1901. Well, I was supposed to go, but my dad died that spring, and I had to assume more responsibility for the running of our hotel, the Clifton House. You've been there, of course, but for the benefit of those who haven't, it is just south of the Union Club on Germain Street at Princess. It is a very busy hotel and very popular with the businessmen that come to Saint John. So my sister Clara, who is not that far from London, read the paper for me. They only gave her ten minutes, and it was a very long and thorough paper, and should have had an hour. You can still read the report in the annual minutes of the council if you would like."

BELDING: "Well, now that your hopes and dreams have come to fruition with the first playground started up right here in Saint John, can you tell us a bit about what was accomplished this summer?"

PETERS: "Be careful how you write that up, Mr. Belding, because some people might come to think of Saint John as being first, but that is not the case. Montreal took up the idea following my presentation and they began programs right away, and they had continuous programs for four summers before we got underway here in Saint John. They now have five programs operating and I think there are others, too, across Canada that took the idea up before the citizens of Saint John got involved. And Mr. Belding, you and your newspapers had a lot to do with it getting going, and being a success, and you should take some of the credit, too."

BELDING: "But the fact remains, Miss Peters, it was your initiative in presenting the idea to the National Council that got it started. You should be proud of that. And I am proud of what we did at the *Telegraph* and *Times* to help."

PETERS: "The money you raised through the public subscription campaign—I believe we got a bit over $1,600, and both your newspapers gave $200—well, that money certainly went a long way to making our summer a success."

BELDING: "Let's talk a bit about that, shall we. Where did you get your staff?"

PETERS: "We were able to get a trained lady from Montreal, Eva Miller, and she was a great help in showing our many volunteers how to conduct the playground programs. Miss Miller has received many compliments for the work she has done. There were four to five hundred children daily for the seven weeks we were open, and we ran programs six days a week. We had four teeters, three large swings, two sets of quoits, two games of ring toss, two bean bag boards, two hundred pails and shovels, two basketball sets, ten baseball sets, one table for clay modelling, two tables for weaving, one sewing circle, and one bead-stringing table."

BELDING: "Quite a variety! In your opinion, what proved to be the most popular activity?

PETERS: "Basketball—and plans are underway to add another court for next year."

BELDING: "I know you had a very special closing. Can you tell us about that?"

PETERS: "We had an exhibition of the children's handiwork—like crocheting, sewing, clay work, woven mats—at the Brussels Street Church and some of this will be displayed at the fall exhibition. At the Centennial grounds, we were able to get Harrison's Band to entertain the children, and Mrs. Chisholm, who played for them every Friday afternoon, was there, too. And the children put on drills and marches, some sang solos or were in choruses, and others did recitations. We had a good crowd of their parents to see them in action, too. Every child received a bouquet of flowers that were provided by local merchants. It was a great day."

Now, up to this point, there was not one bit of information conveyed that could not be backed up by the many reports in the daily papers of the era, some of them no doubt written by Belding himself. However what followed was my imagination at work and the conclusion of the event. And in a way, I hope, it was the tribute that Mabel Peters deserved but didn't receive in her lifetime, or in the years that followed when the local council tried to get her honoured.

To finish the day, I had Belding ask Peters, "Did they give you a bouquet, Miss Peters?"

And she replied, "Why, no, they didn't, but I did not expect any reward. It was all about the children, Mr. Belding, not about me. Why, there were so many that helped so much this summer. The mayor, Mr. Sears, was so helpful, and Joseph Allison, and Mrs. Alice Tilley, and Miss Morton, Miss Burditt, Belle Miller, Miss Stevenson, Miss Scott, Mrs. Chisholm, who did the kindergarten, and Miss Fowlis, who did the clay modelling, and Miss Read, who did the sewing, and I must not forget to mention Mr. Hill, the caretaker at the school, who was so helpful. Oh, I hope I have not left anyone out…that would be awful. Oh, and you, Mr. Belding, with all those kind words and stories in your papers, even some photographs, which I know are so expensive to reproduce, you deserve our thanks, too, Mr. Belding. Do you know they call you 'Great Heart Belding,' for all the good things you do in our community? And your fellow workmen think you do way too much; why, they think running a newspaper is quite enough, but you just seem to have such energy and are always so willing to help, especially when it involves children. I hope we can continue to do this, Mr. Belding, as there is still a great need in this city to be met."

And Belding replied, "You embarrass me with your kind comments, Miss Peters, but I see a young man here with a bouquet, and he's just whispered in my ear that he would like to say a word before we depart the scene of this first playground, so let me call him up here. What is your name, young man, and what is your mission?"

The young man approached carrying a bouquet of flowers, saying, "I am Jeremy Keats and I have come from the year 2006, and as a representative of all the children alive now who still benefit from Miss Peters's founding of the first playground here at Centennial School. I want to correct an oversight of the past. When all those kids got flowers, Miss Peters should have too. So here you are, Miss Peters. Thank you very much for what you have done to benefit children everywhere as a champion of the playground movement."

And Joan Pearce, as Mabel Peters, accepted the token of appreciation, while I, as A. M. Belding, looked on with a feeling that perhaps—just perhaps—Mabel herself was there too!

The next day, a plaque was unveiled by the Leisure Services Department, and "Mabel Peters" and "A. M. Belding" were there once again to bring the past alive. The plaque is in the Allison Grounds and reads:

MABEL PETERS (1861–1914)
PIONEER ADVOCATOR FOR CANADIAN PUBLIC
PLAYGROUNDS
FIRST SAINT JOHN PLAYGROUND ESTABLISHED IN 1906

The Forgotten Story of the First Miss Canada

It is not widely known that the first Miss Canada was a Saint Johner, Winnifred Blair, who was crowned in Montreal on February 10, 1923. Unfortunately, the contest was a financial bust. In addition, there was some backlash from feminist groups that thought the contest exploited women. Montreal decided not to repeat the contest, and no one else took it up. The Depression and World War II were more pressing concerns in the thirties and forties, so the competition was not staged again until 1946. Because of this twenty-three-year gap, Winnifred Blair's story was, tragically, largely forgotten, both nationally and locally.

However, postcards of her posed in front of an ice castle at the edge of King's Square in uptown Saint John brought the matter to my attention. After doing some basic research on the topic, I sent a query letter to the *New Brunswick Reader* asking if there were people still alive who knew Miss Blair, later Mrs. Drummie. I hoped there would be someone who could share first-hand information about her and the role she played as Miss Canada.

I received a half-dozen calls, including one from her son Fred, who said, "Mom didn't talk too much about it." Nevertheless, he was able to share some stories he had heard over the years. He was also able to provide me with a great photo of her in the fine gown she wore at the competition. He told me that the photo was taken for Moirs Chocolates for a special box of candy they produced to mark the event. The photo left no doubt that she was a knockout, but I knew from background reading that beauty was a secondary qualification, as the judges were looking beyond the physical attraction of the ladies, trying to select someone with winter skills to go along with poise and charm. In Winnifred Blair, they found the perfect combination.

Nice as it was to interview her son, it was because of a call from Rev. David Barrett of Sussex that I was able to reach back and hear the story from Blair herself. David had taped an interview with her on the topic just two years before her death on May 24, 1983. At the time of the interview, David was studying at UNB and had chosen as his thesis a study of the first Miss Canada pageant. In outlining his aim he stated, "This paper will discuss the short reign of Winnifred Blair as Miss Canada and examine to what extent she was used as a symbol of regional pride. How did Maritimers feel about Miss Canada? How did she feel about herself? Was she a symbol of Maritime rights? Of woman's rights? Of anything?"

Though David said he had bought the very best tape available at the time of the taping, it had deteriorated and portions of it were not clear. Nonetheless, it still proved to be the most detailed of all the local stories collected. Some of Miss Blair's comments in response to David's questions follow. The brackets are my attempt at editorial clarification.

DB: "I've been doing a lot of reading about you. There was a poem written about you."

WB: "A funny thing: about a week ago, about quarter past eleven, I was watching television, and the phone rang, and it was a man. At first I thought it was Fred as he calls me quite often. He asked me if I was Winnifred Blair. I said, 'yes.' He

Postcard of Winnifred Blair, the very first Miss Canada.

"*Miss Canada*"

asked if I had been Miss Canada. I said, 'yes.' Still nothing from him, so I asked, 'Who am I talking to?' He told me his name, I've forgotten it now. He was in Montreal. He said, 'I was in Saint John when you came home, and Charlie Gorman was there and there was a skating competition and I haven't been back since.' That was fifty-eight years ago. He still didn't tell me what he wanted. The only thing we could figure is that he either had a bet with somebody or a discussion came up and he said 'I'll find out.' So he did. This is funny. This is the second time this has come up [recently] and I don't hear of it for years."

DB: "You were the very first Miss Canada, weren't you?"

WB: "Supposed to be."

DB: "How did you feel when you won?"

WB: "Well, I was quite pleased. I was quite excited. I was only nineteen. We had a week in Montreal. It was put on by the Montreal Winter Carnival.... You were supposed to have a grounding in winter sports, which I did. I skated a lot and was doing almost anything. I was a great friend of Ollie Golding. Her father was a manager of the Imperial Theatre. I was there underfoot one day, and he asked me; 'Would you go over'—they were then getting Miss Saint John, you see—'and go [to represent] for the theatre. I know you can skate.' I said, 'All right,' and went over. It was at the arena then, which is where the Thistle Curling Club is now, the old arena [in the North End of Saint John]. We went over on a Saturday afternoon. I was picked there as Miss Saint John, then they sent me to Montreal, and Mr. and Mrs. Golding went with me. We had a week there. There was a panel of judges—we hadn't met them, they watched, I mean they were in different places. We had skating parties, we were entertained by different clubs—I guess you would call them skating clubs—and we went up to this beautiful toboggan slide on Mount

Royal, you know. We had a party up there and dances. Birks, they had a nice tea room up there. Just a week like that—watch the girls skating and sliding around. Saturday night there was a closing dance in the Windsor Hotel in Montreal. That's when I was picked."

DB: "I know you did a tour of the Maritimes when you were chosen, and from what I have seen you went to Sydney, Halifax, Moncton, St. Stephen. I read the newspapers and there was a lot of talk of you visiting all of Canada. Did you ever do that?"

WB: "No. I'll tell you, the Montreal Carnival, they were supposed to do that and I was supposed to have my picture painted and all this stuff, but they didn't have enough money to do it."

DB: "I also read that at one point they wanted to send you to London to see the Queen. That never came through either?"

WB: "No. It never came through. Another thing I was invited to was Atlantic City to participate in their American one too [the Miss America pageant]. It was overruled by Mr. Golding. He was very adamant about keeping it—well it was supposed to be a real Canadian girl, and he didn't want any commercial input in it at all. I had offers to go and do movies too. In New York I went to a studio [for a test]. I've forgotten what it was, and while I was there I decided not to go [through with it]. So I came home and never did anything about it. I'd had a twelve-page telegram from him [Mr. Golding] the night before. I was in New York and staying with an aunt at the time. I was getting a bit fed up with his interference…. It…got very taxing and I feel sorry for the Queen, as I know a little of what she goes through."

DB: "What my paper is about [is that] my professor says that when you were chosen, this was a time when the Maritimes felt underprivileged to the rest of Canada, so I am tying you in with that aspect. I was wondering, when you were chosen as Miss Canada, did you feel that you were doing something special for the Maritimes?"

WB: "I thought it was to Saint John. That was the information given in the paper. I don't think it would give it a lift in any way. But it did sort of put it on the map. Know what I mean?"

DB: "I know that everywhere you went, big crowds turned out to see you.... I read where the railroads gave you your own private car."

WB: "I think that was just the once. It wasn't very far, that's for sure. [Actually, to Moncton]. I went to Sydney, I went to Glace Bay, and I went to Moncton, and I went to Halifax, quite a few places around the Maritimes. [Also to St. Stephen and Woodstock in New Brunswick, and farther afield to Cleveland, Ohio, for the Gyro Club]. My father had died in 1922. I was working. I just couldn't afford to not work. I wasn't being paid for this. The only thing I got was the city gave me five hundred dollars. [A year's wages at the time—a considerable gift.] I had a brother and a sister who were still going to school. I couldn't really take the year off to do anything. Too boring anyway. My crowning—that was in February, and then I left for New York for a month just for vacation. Then when I came back, I went to work in the Power Commission. I worked there till I was married. They [had] just opened, just started [in 1922]."

DB: "Did they have another Miss Canada the year after you?"

WB: "Never heard of another one, except in Toronto. It was a different manner. It was like they have today. They have a concession of some kind you see. There was another Miss Canada [from Saint John], you know, Judge Higgins's wife, Rosemary [Keenan] Higgins [in 1959]."

DB: "I read in what used to be called *Canadian Weekend Magazine*, an article that said that Miss Canadas always seem to be forgotten. They are famous for a year, and then nobody seems to know what happens to them.... Something that struck me rather strange about this—this article was saying that it was wrong, that they should always be remembered and that the first Miss Canada was chosen in 1946, and it was a shame that she had been forgotten. Here you'd been chosen twenty-three years earlier."

WB: [This part is jumbled badly, but is reconstructed from what David recalled and others confirmed.] "They knew I was first, or some did. They were after me for years to come back. The CBC wanted me on *Front Page Challenge* about the first competition. My husband thought I shouldn't go. He said, 'I don't think you better take the chance of getting hurt. Gordon Sinclair doesn't ask very pleasant questions.' So I didn't go. But I did go [to an event] on my fiftieth birthday. I went to Toronto."

DB: "So you haven't been forgotten?"

WB: "They knew. You know Danny, what's his last name. [It's unclear who she's talking about]. He's in China now. He called me, and I'm telling you, he and the other dandy called me, they were kind of supercilious. One day they called me and asked would I like a little trip to Toronto? Like I was a little old lady from the back-woods. I said, 'No thank you, I just got home from Europe!' That kind of stopped them for a while. Then *Canada AM* called me up and apparently they were going back into the twenties and discovered this story. I said that I would go if they would give me the date I wanted. So I gave them this date, you see, so that when I got up there I went on a half-hour program. It wasn't very much. They asked me [about the first competition]; I talked to them. Afterwards we went in and had breakfast, and while we were at breakfast, I said that it was my birthday. The reason I picked the day was because it is my birthday. They were all cross because I had wanted to have a birthday party and put it on the air. I was just as glad they didn't, though. I'll tell you who was there: Rudolph Penny [name is not clear]. He was on at the same time and I met him. That was more fun for me than going on television. Oh, the odd thing—nice things happened once in a while."

DB: "Did you ever feel that by becoming Miss Canada, you were doing something for Canada?"

WB: "No."

DB: "I'll tell you why I asked that. You were the first woman ever allowed in the coal mines in Sydney [actually Glace Bay]. I also read that you were the first woman ever allowed to sit on the floor of the legislature [in New Brunswick]. That was quite a thing."

WB: "Yeah, that was fun. I just sat on the step, the lower step. That's where I sat."

DB: "When you went to the different places to visit, did you ever give speeches, or were you just there for people to see?"

WB: "No, I didn't give speeches. They invited me and I'd have lunch. That was kind of fun. Sometimes, I'd go to dances, too."

At this point, the tape abruptly ends, though there seems to be conversation under a garbled foreground noise that continues for some time. Too bad!

In later years, Miss Canada put her experiences with public appearances and crowds to good use. She eventually replaced the winter sports of skiing and skating with a summer sport, golfing, and served as the president of the Canadian Ladies Golf Association— another accomplishment for this remarkable Saint John woman.

Grace Darling of the St. Croix

The story of Roberta Grace Boyd's heroic rescue of two Maine yachtsmen during the stormy night of October 8, 1882, is so astonishing that it is almost unbelievable. In fact, I use it frequently when I speak in schools as an example of a story that is so hard to believe, we need corroborating evidence in order to prove that it's not a tall tale. So I usually begin by telling the story, then ask the students how I would go about proving it to be true. I do get some surprising answers.

This is how I often tell the story...

In the days of wooden ships, almost every youngster growing up in New Brunswick knew of a relative who had been lost at sea, or of a lucky one who had almost been clutched by Neptune, but escaped. Such tales were told again and again around the winter fire. Survivors would share stories of heroic acts by those who had perished in storms, thus keeping the memory of the unfortunate victims alive. Most of these stories have been lost as new generations have come along and travel at sea has become safer, though there are still tragedies every year.

One of the most poignant stories of heroism on the Bay of Fundy coast involved a rescue by a twenty-one-year-old woman, and has been all but forgotten even in the Charlotte County area of New Brunswick where it occurred in 1882. It is the story of Roberta Grace Boyd, who became known as the Grace Darling of the St. Croix.

It happened on the night of October 8, 1882, a stormy night, when John Boyd, the lightkeeper at Spruce Point, had gone into St. Stephen to do some business and had left his daughter, Roberta, to prepare the light. This was in the days before electric lights, and it was not an easy job to prepare the lighthouse lamp. She had to clean the lens, pour kerosene into the lamp base, and trim the wick. And to do all that, she had to climb a circular staircase some eight metres high to get to the top of the light station. But she had been well trained by her dad, and that night, though she struggled against the wind to reach the lighthouse, and it twisted and swayed in the gale that was brewing, she accomplished the task without incident. Once she saw that all was in good order in the lighthouse, she started back for home. As she crossed the rustic bridge that led to the point of land on which the lighthouse stood, she thought how lucky she was to have a safe home in which to retreat and wait out the gale.

After supper, she relaxed and read by lamplight with her mother and younger sister by her side. About nine o'clock they were startled by the sound of cries coming from the river in front of the house. Holding the door open in the gale wasn't easy, but they did it in order to peer out across the black, foam-flecked water. They saw nothing, but from time to time, when the wind calmed, they again heard the cries for help, which they judged came from a point nearer the American shore of the St. Croix.

Certain that someone was in trouble out there, Roberta said, without hesitation, "I'm going mother, that could be father out there," and ran down the bank to the boathouse, calling back to her sister to help her launch the boat. Once onto the water, Roberta

Lighthouses are picturesque when the weather is calm but conditions aren't always so wonderful. This is Swallowtail Lighthouse on Grand Manan—Spruce Point is gone!

Grace pulled strongly on the oars, and drove the boat through the raging waves toward the sound of the voices still calling for help.

She was tossed like a cork on the waves but guided by the cries, now fainter and more despairing. After what seemed an eternity, she came upon an upturned sailboat with two exhausted men clinging to it. Roberta reached them just in time, as they could not have kept afloat much longer. With coolness and judgement equal to her courage, she prepared to get the men into her boat. Pushing the stern near one, she managed to pull him in, at which point he collapsed on the bottom of her boat, unable to aid in the rescue of the other. Working her oars furiously, she circled the overturned craft to its opposite side, where the other man was still clinging, and succeeded by an almost superhuman effort in dragging him in over the bow.

Using the beam from the lighthouse at Spruce Point as a guide, Roberta rowed towards home as if her life depended on it. It really did, as now her boat was low in the water and might swamp at any moment in the ever-mounting waves. Finally, she neared the Canadian shore and the beams of the light swept across the boat. One of the nearly unconscious men revived enough to gasp out, "We're saved by a kid, and a girl at that!"

Now, this last part always gets a comment or two from the children in the audience, especially the girls. So I ask them to tell me if they think a young lady of twenty-one could pull off such a mission. Most of them don't think it would be possible. At that point, if I take a vote, usually two-thirds of the class will say I have made the story up. I tell them that in order for me to establish that the story actually happened, I have to have three pieces of evidence that can be used as proof.

What could they be? I ask them.

Some suggest I ask Roberta herself, forgetting that the story happened in 1882. Some say I should ask her relatives, those that have descended from her. I explain that the story could still be fabricated, and that I need hard evidence. Sometimes, they will suggest I find the story in other books. I explain that this could still be just a tale that has been told, and that its appearance in print does not guarantee it is true.

At some point, I tell them that I will continue the tale, and that this continuation should give them a lead as to how we can gather some solid evidence on the matter. So I resume the story...

Soon the two survivors were warmed and fed by Mrs. Boyd, and in a short while they returned to their home over the border in Maine. There, they began to share the story, and it eventually came to the attention of officials from the Canadian government and the town of St. Stephen.

A short while after the rescue, Roberta was presented with a costly gold watch, which bore this inscription: "Presented by the Government of Canada to Miss Bertha [Roberta's nickname] Grace Boyd, daughter of Mr. John Boyd, keeper of Spruce Point light, in recognition of her humane exertions in saving life in the St. Croix River, 8th October 1882." The citizens of St. Stephen complemented the watch with a gold chain. The Department of Marine and Fisheries had a valuable rowboat made for the heroine, which bore upon the stern these words: "Marine and Fisheries, Miss Bertha Grace Boyd, GRACE DARLING OF ST. CROIX, October 8th, 1882." When John Boyd died, Roberta was appointed lightkeeper in his place. No other women of the area had ever held that position, and she remained as the lightkeeper until January 10, 1944, when she died.

At this point, the students will usually jump in to point out that perhaps the watch, or the boat, might still exist. And indeed they do, as part of the collection of the Charlotte County Historical Society in St. Stephen.

In their collection, too, are several yellowed clippings from the *St. Croix Courier* that tell the story of Grace Helen Boyd's heroic rescue. I tell the students that, taken together, these items prove beyond a reasonable doubt that a young lady from Spruce Point really did save two drowning yachtsmen on that stormy night more than a hundred years ago.

Life in Acadie

Ghosts and Christmas in Old Acadie

When I started sharing stories in schools around the province as part of a government program called Writers in the Schools, I came to realize that there had been a fundamental change in the education system since my school days. Almost all of the students I was meeting were in French immersion classes or were at least taking French at a level that would give them some competence in the language. I had a hard time relating stories to these students that were relevant to the culture of the language they were studying.

I knew it was too late in life for me to begin to learn French, so instead I decided I would try to collect as many stories as I could from the Acadians themselves. This did not prove to be as easy as I thought it would be, largely because I do not speak French. But eventually, I met the people you will meet in the stories that follow, people who shared thoughts on a wide variety of topics and enriched my understanding of the Acadian experience in New Brunswick.

The first people who shared stories with me were Jeanne and Clairmont Côté, who responded to a query I had placed in one of my columns asking for Acadian stories. At the time, Clairmont and Jeanne lived in Moncton,

Clairmont and Jeanne Côté with the picture he painted of the Acadieville Church, where his wife attended mass many years ago.

but Clairmont grew up in Saint Arthur, Restigouche County, while his wife was raised a couple hundred kilometres southeast in Acadieville, Kent County. Clairmont's first story immediately convinced me that his consciousness of the world of ghosts and spirits was at a level most of us never experience.

His story began when he was a lad of eight and living at St. Arthur on the province's north shore. The family of twelve children was shocked when their father suddenly died, and it was at that time that Clairmont began having trouble sleeping at night and developed a real fear of the dark.

He requested and was given a coal lamp to light his room. One night before bed he'd been teasing one of his brothers. Later, he awoke in the night, and it seemed his protective lantern was moving toward him and growing alternately brighter and dimmer. Little knowing she was adding to his fears, his mom told him his dad had come back to warn him to stop teasing his brother. A few weeks later, he had a dream in which he saw his dad. It was more like a nightmare, he says now, and it woke him. He was in a cold sweat, with moisture running off his limbs. He sat up and looked around the room. In the dim lamplight he thought he saw his dad in the shadows. He became weak with fear and almost fainted. He cried for help. When it arrived, the shadowy figure he thought was his dad turned out to be a bag of old clothes hanging on a hook, but it served to amplify his fear of the dead and the dark.

When Clairmont was about twelve, this fear was to be deepened further. His sister's first child had died and a pine coffin was made by the family. The child was laid out at home and then at the local church. Clairmont, along with some cousins and other schoolchildren, was chosen to be a pallbearer for the child's burial. It was not an experience Clairmont was looking forward to, but he was assured it was customary to be involved, so he went along with it. He got through the service with no problems, but later the kids at school told him a disturbing fact—the ghost of the buried child would come back that night to thank him for taking part in the burial.

It was with some dread that he went to bed. He lay awake for a long time with the pillow over his head and tried to tune out the world around him. Eventually, he drifted off to sleep. Sometime in the night he awoke from his fitful sleep and saw an angel standing in his bedroom, about a metre from his bed. Her hands were clasped in a prayerful fashion. She looked to be about five or six years old. Clairmont was sure she did not look like his dead cousin, but he was equally sure the angel had come to thank him for burying the child. When the angel came up beside the bed it was too much for Clairmont. He screamed. An older sister came running into the room to comfort him. She tried to rationalize the situation and convince Clairmont that it was a dream and he hadn't seen a real angel, but he knew what he had seen.

After Clairmont related that spooky and gripping story, I asked him and Jeanne if they had any Christmas memories, as I was interested in collecting stories about Acadian Christmas traditions. They really came alive as they began sharing tales of their childhood Christmases in the thirties and forties.

Clairmont's earliest recollections of Christmas are in his seventh year: "We spent the winter in a little log camp, just outside Saint Arthur and about a mile from the main Fred Basque Lumber Camp, where my father worked. There was mother, father, my older brother, and three of my sisters, and we were all in two rooms. In late December, Dad went to town to get some Christmas supplies. We'd go to the bush and get a tree, and we'd make our decorations. We'd use cardboard to make moons, stars, and cover them with foil from the green tea mom had. We had no tree lights, but it still looked good in the corner of the cabin."

Due to the distance to Saint Arthur, the family did not go out to midnight Mass on Christmas Eve, but they did have prayers on the Holy Night. In fact, Clairmont said, "we had prayers every night... said the beads...gave thanks to God."

"Jingle Bells" was one song he recalled singing. "It would be a mix of French and English. I think is went something like 'Père

Noël, Père Noël, bring us some presents some candies and toys,'" he said with a chuckle. There were seldom toys, though, until the war years when they were back living in Saint Arthur. His dad had died, and his older sister went off to work and helped out at Christmas.

But back to the camp. "On Christmas morning," Clairmont recalled—"never Christmas Eve," he stated emphatically—"the stocking we hung would have oranges and apples dad had bought and candies and mittens mom had made."

From the age of seven onwards, Clairmont snared the rabbit for the Christmas dinner. "It was a meat pie, pork, rabbit, potatoes and spices," he explained, adding, "It wouldn't be Christmas without it." Though he no longer uses the trapping skills his mother taught him, he still buys a meat pie every Christmas from Emily's Bakery. "It's not like the wild rabbit but it's sure good."

He'd also buy, if he could, a checkerboard Christmas game he recalls by the name of "Borrow." "It was very popular in the lumber camp, but it's unknown today," he lamented.

He also recalls another diversion called "Whose got the button?" And outdoor play was popular at Christmas, too, with sliding and skiing being his favourites.

Two hundred kilometres away, near Rogersville, his wife-to-be celebrated her Christmas somewhat differently. Jeanne told me, "We decorated our tree just like Clairmont described doing his, and hung our stockings as he did, and waited for Santa. I thought I saw him once but I guess it was a trick, a shadow. About age seven my sister told me all about Santa."

Unlike Clairmont, her family never missed midnight Mass. "We went by horse and sleigh…. We'd be all bundled in robes…. My, it was cold at times," Jeanne said. She added, "While sleighing, we'd sing 'Jingle Bells,' but also church songs like 'Gloria' and 'Venite Adoramus.'"

"Everything was in Latin then you know," Clairmont explained.

After church there would be a feast—but no dancing. "My father didn't go for that," Jeanne said, "though some families danced all night."

The main food at the feast in Acadieville was not rabbit pie, but poutine, which Jeanne described as a mix of raw and cooked potatoes balled around a square of pork or chicken, and then boiled. This treat was unknown in Clairmont's neck of the woods. Also unknown to him was the delight of a battery-powered radio, which Jeanne and her family would enjoy listening to in the dark nights of December and through the winter.

Both Clairmont and Jeanne remember Christmas cards filling hollows in their trees. "Some came from aunts and cousins in the States," Jeanne recalled. Both said cards of the era were very elaborate. "You don't see fancy and glittery ones like that much today," Clairmont said, and Jeanne agreed. Although life was hard at the time for many Acadian families, Clairmont and Jeanne both have fond memories of their childhood Christmases and of those now vanishing traditions.

Lauraine Léger's Acadian Traditions

It was four years before I had a chance to do another interview on the subject of Acadian experiences, and it was well worth the wait when, on April 21, 2004, I met with Lauraine Léger in Moncton. It had been arranged by a Saint John friend, Alice Garner, who was also living in Moncton at that time, and who added a few comments as we went along. Lauraine grew up in Saint Paul, about forty kilometres north of Moncton.

Based on what I had talked about with Clairmont and Jeanne Côté, I began by asking Lauraine about the importance of midnight Mass as part of the Acadian tradition. She thought a bit, slipped into a reflective mood, and said, "The main thing for Acadians at Christmas was the midnight Mass. It was the only time they would go out by horse and buggy at night. It was a few miles for most of them. When they were arriving at the church it was really special. It was lighted and was the only time of the year when they could enjoy an evening ceremony. Besides the lighting there were decorations with the crèche, manger, with trees and everything. They didn't have any at home at the beginning of the twentieth century. Everybody would go see the crèche before leaving the church. The music and the singing, also, they were practising for quite a long time. There were greetings in front of the church when they came out, not like today when people just run to their cars. They were talking and wishing Merry Christmas to everybody. Most of the people I talked to, this is the first thing that they told me about Christmas, midnight Mass. They sang special French hymns, coming from France, the medley of most of them."

She continued, "There was two things. The Grand [High] Mass, the main one, and there were some parts in Latin that were sung. There were two other masses after that. The people didn't leave.

The singing wasn't in Latin. They were French hymns, French tradition. It was accompanied by the organ. Sunday Mass was usually accompanied by the organ, and they had a few people, choirs." She noted that the priest celebrates the Eucharist three times during the evening because there was only one priest in the small villages.

Choir procession prior to midnight Mass at a church in Bathurst.

Among her fondest memories are special bells on the sleighs on these occasions. She explained, "They would even decorate the horse. They had special bells that weren't used at other times. It reminded them of Christmas. Some had red ribbons. The horse was part of Christmastime then."

I asked her about the celebrations following the service, which I believed was called *réveillon* and involved an all-night party. But she informed me that this was "not always done, everywhere. If you go far back enough, many people told me, they were very tired, and they would just go to bed. It might be three in the morning [when they got home]. It was not a big *réveillon*, the beginning of the century, it was tea with a few pastries, things like that. Today it is a real meal, and now it is not midnight Mass, it is a nine o'clock Mass, sometimes a seven o'clock Mass. We have to put it into perspective, it was midnight Mass, and the only time when they were going to church at that time."

I wanted to cover some of the secular parts of the celebration so I asked her whether they had Santa and a Christmas tree.

"Not before the thirties," she said. "It was coming [in then] from outside, from what I've heard. Sometimes young girls going out to the city to work, or even to the States, they would come home or tell their parents what was going on [there], and it started like that with very simple homemade decorations, made from the foil around a pound of tea. They used to keep that and make garland, and use popcorn. If they received cards, they would put a few on the tree. That was about it."

Alice jumped in to add that she had some early cards that were made by her mother's two aunts in Quebec, and she noted, "All of them had religious rhymes, or connotations. I have an image of a wooden shoe with a prayer inside along the back, another image such as a bunch of holly or a tree. They were sent to put on the Christmas tree. They were from nuns in convents in Quebec."

This reminded Lauraine of a story she heard around Cape Bald. "It was in the thirties or forties—the first Christmas tree, at least in this area, the southern part of New Brunswick. This young girl had gone to the States and came back with this idea, she would put up a Christmas tree.... The news spread around. The whole village would come to see the Christmas tree in that house on Christmas day. It was so special for them: a tree—in the house—with decorations!"

As for gifts that would be under the tree, Lauraine explained, "At first, it was the Christmas stocking, the only thing for the children. It was hung in the house, behind the stove. In the morning there was a rush to see what was in the stocking. It was always the same thing: an orange, [which was] special because nobody else in the house had an orange. They just had the barrel of apples in the cellar. A few nuts, a few candies, and if they were rich enough, a barley toy—those were the gifts. They were satisfied with that, they didn't know anything else. When the gifts started—in the thirties, perhaps—they were very simple: a school box, a whistle, maybe a pair of mittens that the grandmother had knitted—very simple things. I remember the first gift I received at Christmas—there was no tree then. My brother was working in Moncton and he bought us each a gift, it was the first gifts to enter the home. Maybe three or four years after that I remember the first Christmas tree. My gift was a brush and a comb for my doll. It wasn't very big. Two or three years after, as I was very young for that little gift, we started to talk about Santa Claus. They told us that you could write a letter to Santa Claus, and maybe he'll bring you something. The first thing that I asked for was a teddy bear. I had a teddy bear. The year after, I was growing older, and I wanted more. I got a little sleigh. It was under the Christmas tree. That was in the late thirties."

As for those letters to Santa, well, Lauraine had a funny story about those. "My father used to drive a bus from home in Saint Paul, to Sainte Marie, Saint Antoine, and on to Moncton. He was going every day. It was a passenger bus. We gave Santa's letter to our father. I suppose that he threw them away. The gift came. So, he must have read it first. We thought he was taking the letter to Moncton. When I was that young I didn't go to Moncton during Christmas. For us,

Santa Claus wasn't in Saint Paul, he was somewhere in the city. Moncton was big for a child."

Though French, Lauraine used the name "Santa Claus," but she added, "In some places they'd call him Père Noël. In some places they used to say it wasn't Santa Claus bringing the gift, it was the newborn Jesus. Their parents used to say that Jesus will bring you something if you're good."

I was surprised when Lauraine told me that skating and skiing were rare when she was a child, and that sleds were homemade. Alice interjected here with a memory from her hometown of Grand Père, where they had made a bowling alley for the boys out on a hillside. "It had a gutter and he had made the ball and the pins. This was for Mom's two youngest brothers, and they'd bowl on this rather makeshift bowling alley out in the fields, and it would get rained on. And when they weren't there, Annette and I would go out and bowl," she laughed.

I was amazed by this resourcefulness—people making use of the simple materials available to amuse themselves and enliven celebratory times. In the same vein, storytelling was a big source of entertainment when Lauraine was growing up, especially around the campfire or the kitchen stove. In her words, "The kitchen was *the* place for storytellers. Any night, any time, depending on the situations, sometimes it was an uncle who would be the storyteller, and all the little children at night they were there. Sometimes it was people passing through the village. Peddlers—some would pass through to fix shoes and share stories, too."

She continued, "Some were very good storytellers. They were recognized. When people heard they were coming, at night, the house was full. The news was sent all over the village, that they were coming. There were two divisions. Fairytales had kings, queens, princesses, giants, fairies, good or bad—good ones would give gifts, and the bad ones would cast a spell. There were also legends, different from fairy tales, usually something local, that had happened where people can figure for themselves where it was. The geography was very important. Some were universal, but they were situating them and naming the persons, and this made them different from normal stories. Many of them had devils in them. Acadians believed in devils, something awful!"

Lauraine remembers one especially popular story about a sorcerer named Old Dollar, which she was kind enough to share with me. "Old Dollar was known as a sorcerer, and we have to remember, for the Acadians, a bad person like that had to come from outside. Some said that he was coming directly from France. He was so bad, according to the sayings, he had even signed the souls of nine of his offspring to the devil. This is how he had all of his power, which was almost limitless. He got this power by giving the souls to the devil. He could do almost anything. He could put a spell on any person who didn't believe like him, and especially those who didn't believe in his power. His daughter was even a victim. She told everybody a secret about him—that he was carrying a frog in his cap....

"They say that he could change himself into an animal—a pig or a dog. And when the teams were going by, he would trip that team and everybody would fall off the sled. The teams were crossing the ice in the winter, and in the spring, they took the bridge, which was longer, and Dollar kept passing on the ice, which was melting, and they say as soon as he had arrived with his horse and buggy, the ice would be turned to water. He was the only one that would risk that. He could also become a ball of fire, a will-o'-the-wisp. He was running around frightening people right on their doorsteps.

"You can imagine that the parish priest wasn't too fond of this. He was hearing all these stories, and he tried to have better feelings, better sentiments, I suppose to convert him. He didn't succeed, and one day this missionary passed by and he asked him if he could do something. The missionary tried, and nothing. Nothing could be done. Dollar pretended the devil was just as good as God, and no way was he going to change his kind of life. That kept on for a while, till the priest decided to tell his parish the he was now giving them the permission to destroy him. Under certain conditions—not with an axe, not with a gun, or if you use a gun, the bullet has to be blessed before. The saying goes that he was poisoned with a *poutine râpée*. That is an Acadian specialty—that ball of grated potatoes with pork inside, that's really Acadian style....

"The priest decided that since a sorcerer couldn't be buried in consecrated ground, he decided to put in the casket a big piece of wood [in lieu of Dollar], so the pallbearers and the parish as a whole would not know. That was carried in the cemetery, but the night before the family members had dug a hole in a field and put the body there. It took a while before everybody knew that. Still it was not over, as he had told those who had not believed in him, 'Just wait and see. Don't believe in me? Just wait till after I'm dead.' Not long after, a few weeks, this hurricane came and started right where the corpse had been buried. It was a terrible hurricane, and tore down the houses, even the church of Bouctouche, the steeple, the church, the harvest, everything perished. It even killed people, injured people, including one Indian woman. That was the last of Old Dollar. They used to say, 'Remember Old Dollar's hurricane?'"

This hurricane was a real one—it happened in 1879 and killed five or six people. But this was the first I'd heard of Old Dollar's role in it—what a wonderful story!

Lauraine concluded her conversation with me by talking about other special days of the year. "Let's start with Valentine's Day," she said. "Of course it started as a love affair, but at the turn of the century here in Acadia it kind of turned ugly. This is when everyone who wanted to play a trick on anybody else, they would use a satirical valentine. You had a very large choice, as in every store in the village they had piles of them, there were sheets with twenty or twenty-five valentines on it, and they could cut it and get quite a few valentines for a few cents. Sometimes it was just to play a joke, to be funny. Others weren't so respectful. If you were a bachelor, a school teacher in an apartment, you could be in the receiving line.... There were cartoons representing an action that a person had made; let's say he had fallen through the ice—you could find a valentine that would illustrate that. A person who was a tattle-tale, she could receive a big face with a padlock. The key was there at the bottom of the sheet, and it would say, 'When you stop talking about people, I'll give you the key.' Anybody could receive anything like that.... Sometimes the people who received it were kind of smiling, others were really hurt.... These had to be anonymous; sometimes people would go to another post office so they would not be discovered. For some, cards were not enough. Certain objects were sent, like a pig's tail, a dead mouse, a rotten apple—this went on till the fifties. Then it turned again to the love valentine with roses and chocolates. For the satirical valentine, we used to celebrate that in school. We had an hour during the day to distribute our valentines, and they were not always nice. It was part of the school tradition."

Next in the year was Lent, about which Lauraine said, "Lent was very long. It was abstinence and fasting, you couldn't eat meat for forty days. Even though they were working, they had to be fasting. This is why, when Easter arrived, it was not what we see today. We had a special meal, and it had to have meat, lots of it! There were no chocolate eggs or rabbits; that is rather recent among Acadians—the late sixties or seventies."

I had always thought that the celebration of the Acadians on August 15 was of fairly recent origin, but Lauraine told me otherwise, saying, "The date was chosen in 1881 at a convention in Memramcook. At that time, I don't think that the people understood the importance of having a national holiday. It was chosen by the Acadian leaders. I would say that certain pastors were more patriotic than others. They would invite a speaker into the parish hall in the twenties and thirties to talk about the Acadians and everything, and it was limited to that. I would say that it started around the fifties that celebrations began, so nowadays it is a very important event in the Acadian celebrations. I would say in 1994 the first Acadian Congress was something as far as celebrations were concerned, and decorations, and people taking part in that. I went through all the villages where all the parishes celebrated through southern New Brunswick, and in all the villages there were decorations. What characterizes the fifteenth of August is the tintamarre. In that parade you make all the noise you can with all the objects you can get in your hands. You have that in many places, it started in Moncton a few years ago. I can tell you that the first time we went on Main Street, not everyone was pleased with us banging pots and pans, but now it is accepted. It is a very old tradition, not only for the fifteenth of August."

To finish out the calendar, I asked about Thanksgiving and Halloween. Lauraine said, "Thanksgiving was not adopted by the Acadians. Even today. There are a few families that have a good Thanksgiving Day meal. During my forefathers' day, [Halloween] wasn't a thing of pumpkins or candies. They used to call it *soir des tours*, or tricks day. Usually there were young men in different groups going around the village, and they would play tricks. It was rural life. They could take the animals out of the barn, they could attach a cow or a sheep to the doorknob. The cow would be pulling to get away when they went to the door. They could destroy small bridges from the houses to the main road. They could move farm machinery for miles. Sometimes they would make a mannequin and they would sit it in the wagon. Sometimes there were farmers who couldn't understand that. They would decide not to go to bed, and it was hard to face those rascals. They would get the worst trick the next year if they happened to say something. It was a mischief night. In the forties they started fires, especially in the north of the province, but not here too often. They used to say that the ghosts were coming to earth, and it grew from that. They were jealous of the living.... They were not pleased to be dead. This is why we as humans are afraid of the dead and the ghosts and all that.... The humans decided to replace the ghosts and then they played tricks, instead of the ghosts."

With that comment, I felt we had come full circle back to Clairmont Côté's ghostly adventures, and the interview closed. I am hugely indebted to Lauraine for having shared with me her wealth of old Acadian stories. After listening to her, I was much wiser for the experience, and I hope you are too.

Searching for Dr. Violette

It is always rewarding to take one of the alternate routes that run parallel to the main highways in the province of New Brunswick. The older roads were not chopped through hillsides; they go over and around them, and in doing so they provided great views of the surrounding countryside. They weave around lakes, dip down to the seashore where waves crash almost onto the roadway; where modern highways commonly bypass towns and villages, older ones go right through them. Thus, they bring you past rustic cabins, delightful diners, and corner stores where the locals used to gather around the isinglass stove, or the checkerboard set up on a barrel of flour, to share stories. Some still do, albeit fewer and fewer with each passing year.

It was when travelling down the Trans-Canada from Edmundston, and realizing that a closer view of the River St. John could be had from parallel route 144, that I came upon the town of St. Leonard, where a filial-topped turret on a Queen Anne revival cottage on the main street

Barbara Mazerolle proudly displays the house her grandfather built while he was the mayor of St. Leonard.

caught my eye. Under a veranda, next to the front door, there was a plaque, which upon closer examination told me this had been the home of Dr. Lorne Violette, the town's first mayor, a beloved doctor, and a member of the Legislative Assembly in the twenties and thirties. It also noted that it was in this home that the first council meeting of the town had been held. I immediately started wondering how many other noteworthy events had occurred in that home, and in the life of this intriguing man, and in the community of which he was a part.

So a quest began. It was amazing how quickly the first bits of information came my way, for just down the street I encountered the Bibliothèque Publique Sr. Lorne J. Violette and, inside, a fine framed photo of the good doctor. A wall plaque noted that he was born on September 7, 1884; got his medical degree at Laval in 1911; married Laura Ouellette in 1913; served in the First World War in England in 1915–1916; was first mayor of St. Leonard in 1920; and served in the Legislative Assembly of New Brunswick from 1922 to 1935. In 1935 he received a medal from King George V, and on October 16, 1938, he died. These were the bare bones of a life well lived, but I knew there had to be more. And there was.

Among the library's holdings there was some background information on his work as mayor. The history of Grande-Rivière noted that in his term from 1920 to 1923 he had the first water supply lines constructed in the town, and also got the fire and police services underway. A church history provided a photo of him driving a very ancient car, another of him peering intently into a microscope, and a third of him holding his daughter Jocelyne in July 1927.

I was eager to find out more, but my limited French was a handicap. Dr. Violette's granddaughter, Barbara Mazerolle, still lives in the area, so I paid her a visit. She told me that throughout her life she has met people time and again who have spoken of her grandfather and the medical care he gave to the families of the area. "I've been told when he started his practice, he still travelled by horse and buggy, and he would go almost anywhere to make house calls if someone was sick. People have told me he would go even when he knew there was no chance of getting paid. Others have told me they paid him with chickens," she said with a chuckle.

She said the family still has some of the medical instruments he used, along with some of his old dishes and china, but most everything else from his house is gone.

She brought my attention to some information on her grandfather in a 2006 calendar issued by the Société culturelle de Saint-Léonard, including a cover photo of his home, which had first caught my eye. From this calendar I learned that his wife, Laura M. Ouellette, was born in Frenchville, Maine, and died on May 2, 1966. I also learned some interesting details of his service in the First World War: that he served on the ship *Missanabie*, spent time at a base in Folkstone, England, and in July 1916 participated in the amputation of a soldier's leg. His death is noted as having occurred on October 16, 1938, when he was just fifty-four.

So a bit more of the life of Dr. Violette came to the fore. I was especially intrigued by the entry for June 3, which mentioned his election to the legislature for the first time. Anyone who is elected as a member of the legislature, and who speaks when the house is in session, has his words recorded for all time in the *Synoptic Reports* of the proceedings of the Legislative Assembly, of which the Saint John Regional Library has a vast collection. They are so dried out from years of sitting on the shelves of Canada's oldest library that I was surprised to be able to use and copy them.

Copies of the reports for the years 1923 to 1934 provided further glimpses of Dr. Violette's life, and give a good idea of how he represented his people during that period. His first speech was to be the seconder of the speech from the throne for 1923. In this speech, he said, "I am glad to note...the government's intention to try to do something to help the farmers" and went on to say that, because he represented a district where most of the inhabitants were farmers, he had "been an eye witness to the difficulties with which they have met." He felt that something had to be done to "keep them on the farms." He suggested that help be given to market their products, and also that the farmers be encouraged to try other crops beside potatoes.

He also noted that "having travelled in many provinces of the Dominion and in several States of the American Union," he was glad to be able to say that "our roads compare well with others I have seen." He spoke in favour of a reduction in railway freight rates, and hoped the government would work toward the inclusion of the Valley Railway into the national system, as it is "a burden on the finances of this province."

As a medical doctor, he was concerned with the alarming spread of venereal diseases everywhere, noting, "This province, unfortunately has had its share." In the course of this speech, he also provides further information on the travels alluded to in the earlier speech. He speaks of visiting "Miami, the magic city, where it is always June, St. Petersburg, the city of perpetual sunshine," and the "annual State Fair in Tampa," where, he complained to the minister of agriculture, he saw not a "single picture of Eastern Canada's [farms] and especially none of this province."

He also spoke in favour of the Musquash hydroelectric project, "developed under trying circumstances," and reminded the house that Grand Falls, in his riding, was second only to Niagara in its potential for power generation. He recommended that it be developed for the "upper portion of New Brunswick."

In 1925 he had less to say. In fact, he rose to speak on only two subjects. In one speech, he called the province backward in its development of roads to aid colonization of the land. In a second, he made another plea for development of Grand Falls saying, "Every weekend when I return home people ask me, 'what about Grand Falls.'"

In 1927 he made an important speech about a subject of much interest to his Acadian constituents. He began by noting with regret that not all of the honourable members understood his language, and then made a plea for the establishment of French-language training for the province's schoolchildren. He argued, "Such knowledge would produce better feeling and understanding between the two great racial elements which make up the province."

His other comments that year included congratulating the honourable member for Saint John (Harrison) for speaking French when making his comments, and Premier Venoit for his road policy, which caused him to be known as "Good Roads Venoit." He again commented on the Grand Falls development, which by then had occurred. He noted that it had been hoped the project would result in more industry in the upper valley, but to date this had not happened, and the "Saint John Valley again was the goat."

Of course, medical matters were always on his mind, and in 1928 he pointed to the establishment of a Red Cross outpost hospital in St. Leonard as a positive move, and one much appreciated by the public. He noted that 104 patients had received treatment and only 4 had died in the past year.

In 1930, he prefaced his remarks in English with a preamble in French, which was not translated. He talked about the need to better support agriculture, as "agriculture is the basis of all industries and the means of keeping young men on the land of their forefathers," adding, "our young people should be encouraged in every way to remain in New Brunswick which is one of the best, if not the best of all the provinces."

In 1931 it becomes clear that Dr. Violette was a Christian man, and well versed with the Bible, for in his speech he concludes a debate on government procedure over the roll call and makes a dig at the government by quoting the Good Book: "There may be salvation for sinners if they repent and atone for their misdeeds, but the boastful, the mighty and the proud are beyond redemption."

In 1932 Dr. Violette spoke for the abolishment of polling booths, "as their maintenance adds to the cost of several candidates," and he came out against the common practice "to supply automobiles, ginger ale, chocolates, and so forth" at the polls—a practice that is thankfully no longer tolerated today. His humorous side is seen at this session, too, when he chides the minister of public works for buying a thirty-five-dollar pair of scissors for a ribbon-cutting ceremony at a new highway, saying, "I am the owner of a pair and would gladly place them at his disposal."

His last recorded comments came in 1934, when he spoke against granting a full dentistry license to several men who had been practicing illegally for nine years in the province, and took umbrage with the government's liquor policy, which they claimed was controlling the use and abuse of the product, but which he dismissed as nonsense. With biting wit, he said, "I come from the driest county of the province, except on the occasion of the last by-election. If it was thought bootlegging was over, I would advise those who thought so to watch the Maine and Quebec borders."

And so we can see from the *Synoptic Reports* that the good doctor was well aware of what went on in and around his St. Leonard home, and was not afraid to speak his mind. More than that, through all of the various documents Dr. Violette left behind, we catch a glimpse of the concerns, passions, and way of life of an Acadian community in the early part of the twentieth century.

I would have to say that my detour into St. Leonard was worthwhile, as are most that one can take in this diverse and fascinating province.

A Kent County Tragedy

Among the older folk I visit in Saint John are Susie and Gerry Gigou, both in their mid-nineties now. Seldom have I gone to visit without hearing a story about their earlier days living in the Acadian heartland of the North Shore. I love these tales of home and school and the hardships of the winter; of travelling through spring mud; of the train trips they took; of the Christmases they celebrated.

On a visit at Christmastime 2005, I heard the most amazing story that they had ever recounted. It was Gerry, usually not as talkative as Susie, who brought out the story that day, and he could have knocked me over with a feather when he did. He said, "You know, David, I never actually knew my father, I was just five weeks old when he died in a skating accident."

Sensing a story, I immediately perked up and asked Gerry to tell me what happened. "Start at the beginning," I said, and he did.

"I'm ninety-five now," he said. "I was born in 1912 in the little village of Saint Louis de Kent in Kent County, the last of a family of six, two of whom were born in Maine when the family lived over the line."

He continued, "All my life I've heard family stories about my dad's early life, but I never met him. Dad came over to Canada from France in 1892, when he was just a boy of fourteen. Some family members believe he came as a stowaway on a ship that had left Brittany. It is also thought he came with another boy about the

Gerry and Susie Gigou are full of great stories.

same age, and there is some conjecture that the boy may have been a brother, but if he was, the brother disappeared and there was no further contact with him. Dad, whose name was Louis, came by the boat into Richibucto, and when it docked it was dark, but the boys set out across the countryside looking for a safe place to stay. I guess that is why there is some thought they were stowaways. Anyway, they looked over the land, and they had no idea where they were, so decided to go their separate ways and try to find a family who would take them in. Dad went north and saw a house that looked promising, and knocked on the door and asked for some food and a place to sleep. He ended up staying there and marrying one of the daughters of the Robichaud household."

Gerry took a breath, then continued. "He found work in the mills of the area, and sometimes had to go off to Maine for work. Wages were about $175 a year and that is what the family lived on. By 1912 the family was living in St. Louis de Kent, and that is when I came along, born on November 27, 1912. At Christmas that year, Dad, Louis, skated up the Kouchibouguac River to pick up Christmas presents for the family. Skating was a common way to get around in winter. He got the gifts, and started back for St. Louis de Kent, but hit an open spot in the river and fell into the water. He managed to crawl out to the shore, but it was very cold, and he could not get a fire started to get dried out and warmed up, and froze to death on the shore. His body was found the next day by searchers. His wife never remarried."

"Wow, that is some sad story," I told Gerry.

"Well, what I wondered," he said, "is would there be any way to find out if the story is true. Now, I have no reason to believe it isn't, but I always wondered if it might have been in the papers."

"I will have a look," I promised Gerry, and a few days later I was able to report that I had found a story that sure looked like it was the story he had told me—but with one startling difference: the name of the victim of an accident is Louis Pugi, not Louis Gigou.

This is the report published in the *Moncton Daily Times* of December 26, 1912:

Kent County Man Frozen to Death
Louis Pugi Broke Through Ice on river and Got Out again, but perished from Cold
Rexton, NB—Louis Pugi, a native of France, and for some years past a resident of Guimond Settlement, near St. Louis, was found frozen to death in the Kouchibouguac River this morning. He left his home Saturday evening to skate up to the village, a few miles distant, and as he was in the habit of staying at night with friends nothing unusual was expected, but as he did not return Sunday, a search was begun this morning, when the body was found. It was evident that he had broken through the ice and got out again, but being wet and exhausted, he perished with the intense cold. He leaves a wife, who was Miss Robichaud of St. Louis, and several children. He was about thirty years of age.

As I read the piece to Gerry, his eyes opened wider and wider. I'm not sure he realized the name change, but Susie did. "Who did you say that was about?" she asked.

"Louis Pugi," I replied, and I probably didn't do a very good job of pronouncing it.

"That has to be Dad," Gerry said.

"Couldn't be anyone else," Susie agreed.

"But how did they get his name wrong?" they both asked almost simultaneously.

"Here's what I think," I responded. "The story must have been phoned into the Moncton paper from Rexton, and the correspondent was misunderstood as far as the name is concerned. Everything else is just as Gerry has known it, the trip from France, Miss Robichaud, the skate on the river, getting out on the river bank—it's all there, so it has to be an error in the name, probably a language problem."

I gave Gerry the clipping, happy to have helped bring some closure to this tragic Christmas story.

Egbert McGraw, New Brunswick's Christmas Tree Boy

Like a lot of people, I've enjoyed many of the very popular *Chicken Soup for the Soul* books. Though most of the stories reflect on experiences south of the border, I was surprised and delighted to find that one of the stories in *Chicken Soup for the Christian Family Soul* has a New Brunswick connection. It's titled "Our Christmas Tree Boy" and it tells the story of one Egbert McGraw of Légère Corner, New Brunswick, who in 1961 tied a letter to a Christmas tree that found its way to a couple in Detroit. That letter not only got him a new pair of skates from the childless Detroit couple, but also resulted in them making a visit to his remote North Shore community the following summer and then sending him Christmas presents for several years thereafter. He later followed up with a trip to Detroit to see the couple who called him their "Christmas Tree Boy."

It's a great story, but written from an American point of view by Edward and Joyce Beckwell of Detroit. I wondered if it might be possible to do the story from the point of view of Egbert. As he was eight in 1961, I felt there was a good chance he would still be alive, but there was also a good chance I might not be able to find him. And even if both parts of the puzzle fell into place, he might not be willing to talk about the story. But somehow it all worked out fine. I have to thank fellow writer Gail McMillan of Bathurst for help in finding Egbert, whom she located in Moncton. He replied to my mail enquiry with enthusiasm, and agreed to meet me in his home to share his story.

To illustrate how lucky I was in stumbling across this story, let me provide some context. In 1961, 1,177,000 Christmas trees were exported to the United States from the Maritimes, with about twenty-five percent—perhaps 300,000—of them coming from the Chaleur area of New Brunswick. As far as he can recall, Egbert placed only one note on one of those trees, with no idea where it would end up or who would read it—if anyone. What are the odds that the man who read and answered it would turn out to be a writer, who at age seventy-four, thirty-nine years after the incident happened, would submit his story to the *Chicken Soup* editors...and that of all the stories they receive, it would be selected for publication...and that of all the stories they publish, I would see this one?

Quite incredible, I think, that this story can now be told from the point of view of the boy of eight who first attached that letter, and who is today a lecturer in accounting at the University of Moncton.

This is what he said the night I met him in Moncton: "In 1961 I was living in what is now called Portage River, but at that time you called it Légère Corner. It is on the North Shore of New Brunswick about seven miles from Tracadie. Compared to today, at that time it was what we would call primitive living. No plumbing in the house, just a water pump that we would prime, but that was the way of life then, and we were happy. We thought we had everything at that time. In the fall, the potatoes and carrots were in the basement, and we had grown two pigs to kill, we had a wood stove and some wood for the winter, and some paraffin for when the electric power went down. We thought we were rich."

In describing his school, Egbert said, "There were six grades in two rooms, and there were two teachers at the school. There was no toilet, no running water, and there was a stove, or sort of a stove, as it was a big tub with wood in it, so the students that were near that were burning, and the ones at the other end were freezing."

One of Egbert's favourite places as a youth was in Pokemouche, where his aunt kept house for a priest. "It was a big house. It had central heating with hot water, and real full bathrooms. My gosh, to be honest, I do not like to say it, but at home we had slop pans for the night," he said with a laugh. He added, "I was spending my summer there, and every weekend I could. It was so nice to be able to sleep at night without having six or seven blankets on your bed."

Summing up conditions in 1961, Egbert said, "What I have described was normal, and everyone lived as we did. And we were rich, because we had food and heat and light. My grandfather was making sure that we always had some wood for the winter, so he was cutting that in early fall. We always had wood one year in advance. Yes, if you had that you were rich people. Grandfather also had an old car, not many did, but he always had a car. Sunday morning during the winter my mother was coming and people were coming and just sitting at the back [of the car], and there might have been six, seven, eight people in the back."

About the letter that brought the first of many changes to his life, Egbert said, "I think that many people had done that before I did it, and I guess I heard about it, and decided it was a way to get a gift at Christmas."

As an aside here, in reading the papers of that era, I found two other incidents of youngsters who attached letters to trees and got responses. The most interesting was about Amber Connors and was carried in the *North Shore Leader* of Newcastle on December 22, 1961. It read:

A note placed on a Christmas tree in Quarryville during the shipping season by a 9 year old Quarryville girl has ended up in Houston, Texas. About 2:30 o'clock Wednesday morning, Mayor D. A. Adam received a long distance telephone call from Byrne Toucheck of Houston saying he had found a note asking for a doll for Christmas signed by Amber Connors of Quarryville, New Brunswick. He was asking Mayor Adams to look into the matter and see if there were such a child. Mr. Toucheck asked Mr. Adams if he were the Mayor of Quarryville, as he did not know the size of the place or anything about it. Mayor Adams had telephoned on Wednesday and located Amber Connors, daughter of Mr. and Mrs. Andrew Connors. The little girl said she had put a note on a tree in a carload of trees on the railway tracks ready for shipment. She had not told anyone about doing this until news of the note's arrival in Texas was received. Mr. Toucheck suggested to the mayor that he present the girl with a doll for Christmas.

The other story involved a boy in Quebec who did the same thing, and who also got a response. There is also a rather well-known story by children's author Natalie Savage Carlson titled "The Letter Upon the Tree," which is about another Quebec boy named Bébert Caron.

Egbert, however, did not know of these stories, though he had heard of a neighbour from Brantville, a young girl, who received a response to a letter, and actually moved to Detroit to live with the couple. She lives in Detroit to this day.

Soon after Egbert's letter-writing escapades, the tree shippers placed security guards at the shipping yard to prevent notes from being placed in the trees. It would still be easy enough to place a note before the trees reached the shipping yard, as most trees were cut by private landowners like Egbert's grandfather and sold to the shipper. Nonetheless, placing notes in Christmas trees is a part of the lore of New Brunswick that is no longer practised, as far as Egbert knows.

"Conditions have changed so much," he says. "People don't live as simply as we did. Times have improved. People expect more and they have more. Louis Robichaud was a great leader and he did a lot for the North Shore—not just the French, either, but for everyone. The North Shore is not like it was, that is for sure."

Egbert continued, "One of the ways it has changed the most is that everyone has Mastercard and that sort of thing and there are so many stores. You got to remember, at that time, there was no general store, no Canadian Tire, nothing. There was a Five and Ten, we were looking at Eaton's catalogue and saw lots of things there we could not buy around home."

Skates were one of those things that Egbert thought he would like to have. And a note on the tree just might make it happen. However, there was an obstacle to overcome. At the time, he spoke and wrote only French, so he had to have a letter written for him. He can't recall if it was his grandmother or aunt who wrote the letter, but this is how it read: "I am a little boy 8 years the 4 of December.

I hope you think of me on Christmas day send me something for my Christmas. I like to have a pair of skate No 3. please tell Santa to come here and don't forget me."

Christmas came that year, and Egbert did not receive the skates. Though Egbert had no way of knowing it at the time, the recipient of his letter was trying very hard to find a pair of skates, and equally hard to find out just where Légère Corner was. Egbert says that he was not disappointed at the time, as "Christmas was as usual, we were still rich. We had a lot of aunts who were generous, we had a lot of food. My grandmother, two or three weeks before Christmas, she was cooking like crazy, filling baskets of cookies and cakes. As I said, if you had food and it was warm in the winter, and you had some paraffin—every year you had to make sure you had five gallons of paraffin for emergencies—all was good."

Santa Claus was part of the tradition too, as Egbert recalled. "I remember when Santa Claus was coming to the city hall. My gosh, we would have a few candies, have fun, we would be waiting for a few hours to get some candy. And there was another Santa Claus in Tracadie, so there was Santa Claus all around looking a bit different."

Santa didn't bring those skates in time for Christmas 1961 as Egbert had asked, but they were on their way a couple of days after Christmas. And when they arrived, it was an exciting time in Légère Corner and at the McGraw household.

"I was real surprised to have something from the mail," Egbert said, "to have it boxed in the mail, and for the skates, but especially from where it came, Detroit. My brothers and sisters, they were surprised too. I have four brothers and four sisters. I am the fifth, right in the middle. I don't think anyone knew, at that time, where Detroit was. It was outside New Brunswick and Quebec, that's all we knew."

The skates did not come out of the box for a long time, and were carefully kept and shown to anyone who came around to see them as the story got around. In fact, Egbert recalls not using them for a long time, and he can't remember where they were first used.

But they were used in time. As he tells it, "I remember we were skating around the house, because there was some melted snow, and when we got older we went in the lake in the woods. Then when we were a little older, we went on the river, then we went to the skating rink, which was more for adults. We were getting up on Saturday morning and walking to the river and putting on our skates and skating until the night, until we could not see the puck. Sometimes we did not have a puck, and we were using what we had—for the goals, we used two chunks of ice. We had fun. We were never the same team, always dividing during the day. It was fun."

When I first talked with Egbert, he was sure the skates were still somewhere in one of his aunts' or cousins' homes. But when I arrived to do the interview, hoping to take a photo of him holding the skates, he informed me that as far as he could find out, they were passed down through the family and eventually lost in a house fire.

However, he did have other mementos, most notably an album of photos of Christmas at the McGraw house, visits to the rectory, and other North Shore and family scenes that nicely brought to life his story. Most were black and white, but a few were in colour, and these, he explained to me, were from the Beckwells, and had been taken when they came to New Brunswick to visit their "Christmas Tree Boy" the following summer.

Egbert explained that visit, saying, "They came in 1962. We had a call, and I think they were down in Newcastle. They said that they wanted to know how to get to our place, we knew they were coming. We had a phone. It was a crank up—one ring, two ring—we were all on the same line. They arrived in a blue Chevrolet convertible. We were able to fit all the family in the back seat, so we were driving on Main Street in Portage River. There were no seatbelts, and it was a convertible. It was major activity down there. People were amazed."

The Beckwells stayed for just one afternoon, but met his whole family. Through the years, they continued to remember him each Christmas, sending him many cherished gifts, including a Roy Rogers cowboy suit, which was his favourite gift of all. "It had two guns and some bullets that go round the belt. That impressed more than the skates—playing cowboys in the woods, and the chaps and the shirt. I still have part of that," he told me.

The Beckwells never came back to the North Shore, but he did see them again when he visited their part of the world. Egbert explained, "We kept in contact with letters [he had gradually learned English over the years], and they were always asking about my mother. I'd been raised by my grandfather and my mother, because my mother had been very sick. I think she impressed them because she looked sick. My dad wasn't around much."

During his university years, he lost contact with the family, but in a strange twist of fate, in a story that already has many improbable moments, he once again had an opportunity to see the Beckwells in the late 1970s, and took advantage of it. He explained, "When I started teaching at the university in Moncton, I had a meeting in Windsor, so I said, 'Why not go see the Beckwells?' I remember we stayed one night in Windsor, and we took the tunnel to get to Detroit. We did not call before. I remember Detroit at that time—oh my, plywood in all the windows. North Shore was better than that!"

Continuing, he said, "We drove through to Lake Shore, Michigan, a small community. I saw the number, so I stopped there, rang the bell and a tiny lady answered the door. When I saw her [as a child], I was small, and she was tall, not tiny. I said, 'Is Mr. or Mrs. Beckwell here?' She said, 'Mr. Beckwell is not here.' I said, 'I'm Egbert.' She nearly fell on the floor. She said, 'Don't say nothing, I'm going to call Ed.' Ed was Irish, so he was taking his beer with his friends. She called him and said, 'Come home, I want to show you something. Come home, you need to come and see.' So he came, and when he saw my car and plate and when he saw me, he said, 'My gosh, you're Egbert!' He invited us to go out to a restaurant to eat, and the next day we invited them to Windsor for a meal. So we had a very nice weekend."

Edward Beckwell has since died, but Joyce is still alive, and as a result of renewed interest in this story, Egbert is going to contact her once more. And when he does, there may be a postscript to this most incredible story of New Brunswick's Christmas Tree Boy.

Not of This World

Kent County Has a Yahoo

From 1998 to 2002 I published ghost stories in the *Moncton Times and Transcript*, entertaining readers with supernatural tales from across the province. Many people sent in interesting stories for my consideration, and of these perhaps the most interesting was the one sent my way by Dan Easter of Bass River, Kent County. He called it "The Yahoo of Kent County in 1910."

In the early 1900s in Kent County, unexplained sightings and sounds in the woods were labelled as "yahoos" and were the main topic of conversation

The Kent County Yahoo is caught frightening Frances Helyar.

around the forge in the old blacksmith shop, where on stormy days the local farmers, lumberjacks, and others gathered to tell yarns that made even some of the bravest scurry for home before the sun went down and darkness set in.

At the time, Tom Ward ran a lumber camp ten or twelve miles up the river that was only accessible by a narrow wagon trail through the dense forest. About every second Saturday, Tom knocked the crew off early, hooked the teams up to the wagons, and took them all out to the settlement, returning Sunday afternoon.

One Saturday Bill Cook's home brew was just nicely ripe and it seems he may have drank a gallon or two too much. Anyway, he missed the wagons going back to the camp. He decided to walk. It was a sunny, warm July afternoon, and after a couple of hours walking, Bill was tired and ill. He stepped off of the trail to a warm dry spot for a rest. When he awoke it was dark, and he couldn't find the trail. He panicked and began running about screaming for help.

Back at the camp, they heard the screams. Instantly they knew it had to be a yahoo, one of the worst terrors of the woods. They ran to the stable, hitched the horses to the wagons, and galloped toward home and safety. When they were passing the spot where Bill was, he screamed. Someone on a wagon yelled, "Faster, it's gaining on us. It's a yahoo for sure."

Bill could find the trail now, and he figured if there was a yahoo it was chasing the wagon. So he headed for the camp. Where, by the way, they had just unloaded two weeks' worth of supplies for ten men.

When the crew reached the settlement they scrambled from the wagon and raced into their homes and barred the doors, completely terrified. They loaded their shotguns and listened at the windows for any sign of the yahoo, until daylight when they gathered at the blacksmith shop and discovered Bill was missing. They figured the yahoo had got him for sure. Poor Bill, what a horrible fate. There wasn't a dry eye in the shop. The tales of the great things he had done were told by each man in turn, some partly true, but most imaginary. No one dared to venture up the trail to the camp, lest they meet the same fate as Bill.

A few days later, a memorial service was held. The preacher droned on and on about what a kind, generous, upstanding citizen Bill had been. Some of the mourners wondered whether it was Bill Cook he was talking about.

A week or so later, Bill decided that if the crew wasn't coming back in, he would go out. Blackflies, mooseflies, horseflies, and mosquitoes were uncommonly thick that year. In an effort to keep from being eaten alive, Bill took the cheesecloth that the cook wrapped the bread in, draped it over his head, and made his way down the trail to home, the cheesecloth floating gently down to about his knees.

The sun had gone down when he reached the settlement, but there was a full moon. Suddenly there were terrified screams, "It's a yahoo, it's a ghost!" Doors slammed, shutters closed, the church bell rang, dogs howled, somewhere a rooster crowed, scaring Bill near out of his wits. He ran to the nearest door and knocked, yelling, "It's me, Bill, let me in!" The trembling reply was "go away, you're a ghost, you're dead, go to your reward."

Now, worse still, he could see a crowd of people coming with torches, clubs, shotguns, pitchforks, and the preacher carrying a large cross in the lead. Fearing for his life, he raced back up the trail toward the camp. A few volleys of shotgun fire were heard, but Bill was too far away and travelling too fast for the shot to reach him. He tore off the cheesecloth so that he could make better time and be less visible. He made the trip back to the camp in record time still wondering why everyone wanted to kill him.

The next day at the blacksmith shop, there were tales of how the buckshot had gone clean through the yahoo, doing no harm at all, and how the creature had vanished into thin air. People also mentioned the smell of brimstone and the fear of the yahoo returning.

Back at the camp, Bill figured he could never go home with the whole settlement out to kill him. He let his beard grow, also adding some weight from the ample supply of food at the camp. After a couple of months passed, Bill made his way back through the woods to the railway track, and walked up it a few miles. When the Limited came along he flagged it down and rode to the station, where he alighted from the train and announced he was Jim Cook and had come from the West to visit his brother Bill. After breaking the sad news to him that his brother Bill had died, they showed him to Bill's cabin. No one ever guessed his true identity.

When the tales at the blacksmith shop turned to yahoos, ghosts, and how Bill Cook had met such a terrible fate, Jim (really Bill) would ease to a dark corner of the shop and chuckle to himself, adding "amen" to all the sympathy heard.

As a postscript, I should mention that this story became one of the basic stunts I would use on Walk 'n' Talk programs for the next few summers. Usually, I would arrange for someone to be in the woods near enough to my walk route that they could hear me as I told the story of the yahoo. They would be draped in cheesecloth; at my signal they would let out a few blood curdling "yyyyaaaahhh-hoooo" yells and come charging out of the forest. It certainly startled more than a few of the participants. On one occasion, however, the yahoo came charging out of the woods before I had given the signal, and ruined the stunt. But when I heard why, I couldn't really be too upset: while my yahoo was waiting, he was joined by two skunks. Apparently skunks have no fear of yahoos, and cheesecloth is no match for the skunk spray!

To this day, I am grateful to Dan Easter, and to all those who shared the province's ghost stories with me and have helped to keep these stories alive.

The Ghosts and Devils of Johnville

Over the years I've heard many great stories from Frances Cullen of Johnville, and from the fascinating people I've met through her. Frances draws in people from as far off as Grand Falls to the north, Presque Isle to the west, the Miramichi to the east, and Saint John to the south. I'm usually the only one from Saint John, though that isn't always the case, and sometimes people have come from much further away—as far as Alberta and New England.

They come to the Saturday night gatherings in her kitchen, not only for her delicious foods, of which her donuts get the most raves, but also because she knows so many interesting people who have delightful stories to share.

One of those who never misses is D. C. Butterfield of Kilburn, the Prison Poet, so-called because he worked as a prison guard for many years. His motto hangs outside his doorway of his neat home a few miles from Perth Andover; it reads, "Have Pen, Will Write," and he does just that. He is a tireless collector of folk tales and historic happenings from the valley and has likely introduced me to more characters than anyone else except Frances herself. Dean is not a bit stingy with his stories, and often encourages others to share with me those they have shared with him.

Among those is one about the Monquart River, which flows into the St. John River at Bath. D. C. has done up the story as poetry and titled it "The Monquarter and the Devil":

There is a legend from long ago about the region down around Bath.
The time the devil stopped up short when Monquart lay in his path.
It happened before my grandad's time,
even before Mike Keenen had his store
Close by the barber shop, and fishermen lined the shore.
A blacksmith shop still met a need, the old hospital stood on Main,
Churches were almost always filled, to the Monquarters life was plain.
He walked his land with head held high
through winter's cold and summer's hot.
His reputation spread far and wide,
known as the very toughest of the lot.
Why even the Devil trembled then was about to tuck his tail and run
When up stepped a strapping man by the name of Giberson.
He took the Devil by the hand, the fellow being quite the sport.
T'was the only way, the legend goes,
the devil would pass thru ole Monquart.

D. C. also provided some humorous context for this story: "The Monquarters and the Tobiquers always had this rivalry. It was always known that Monquarters were so tough that the devil wouldn't even walk through Monquart. When he came to the area he had to get one of the Giberson boys to lead him through. They were always bragging how everything was always great at the Monquart, and Tobiquers did the same about their river. This one traveller got tired of hearing about how big and tough everyone was in Monquart. The Tobiquer began one day to tell about his potato farm. He claimed he had a huge operation and bragged about all the acres he'd planted. He said, 'One day, I got into my car to try to drive around it. I drove all that day and all that night, and it was the next morning before dinner when I got back to the house. What do you think of that?' The Monquarter replied, 'I had a car like that once and I got rid of it!'"

Now, Frances herself has told me no end of stories, including a dandy one about the devil and how he came one night to play cards with some of the local boys at a camp on the North Johnville Road. The devil was, of course, dressed as they were, and they had no idea who they were playing with. This stranger seemed normal enough, except that he was winning all the money. On this night the parish priest decided to pay a visit to the card game, having been tipped off by the men's wives that they were spending a little too much time at cards and way too much time away from home. When the priest entered the camp, he was invited to join in the game by those who knew him, but the stranger did not welcome him. In fact, he took strong exception to the priest's presence, and bolted from the camp. He did not bother to use the door, but went straight through the

wall! As if that was not enough to convince the men they had Satan as a card player, his cloven hoofprints burned into the floor, and he left a lingering smell of brimstone as he departed the little cabin. They gave up the card game without a word from the priest.

Frances also loves to tell the story of an abominable snowman spotted in the area by some of her long-time friends and by her

Frances Cullen in front of her big farmhouse with Don Hemmings.

son Kevin. One winter morning, Kevin arrived at the house saying he'd seen a creature that looked like a man with ivory-coloured hair covering his body. He wanted his .22 rifle in case he saw it again. Off they went. As Frances said, "I had to see what he was raving about." However, she saw only the footprints in the snow at the foot of Dooly Hill. Examining the depressions, she could see that the creature had jumped out of a tree, went across the road eight steps, and then went back up into the trees. "The snow was knocked out of the trees and the steps were shaped something like an axe head," she said. There was eight or ten inches of fresh snow on the ground at the time, which made reading the tracks possible and left no doubt in Frances's mind that the many sightings in the area were not imaginary.

When she tells that story, you're convinced that it has to be the truth, but not all strange sightings in the area have been. Frances can laugh at herself and her family foibles, as evidenced by the following story about her husband and just a little too much whisky.

"There was a story going around about a ghost in the Johnville graveyard," Frances explained. "Mrs. Riley was the first one who mentioned it to me. She came up for the mail. She asked me if I had heard tell of anything strange happening in the graveyard. I said, 'No.' She said, 'We were coming home around half past two the other night and there was a dead man that got right up and walked around.' She added, 'Three or four other people told us this too, about the ghost of the graveyard that they had seen on their way home from the dance following the Johnville picnic.'"

Frances continued, "When I said 'no,' I really meant it. I knew of an incident in the graveyard that my husband Peter was involved in, but I didn't think it would have led to a ghost story. But upon thinking of it, I can see how it might have. What happened was that Peter worked at the harvest supper and the picnic. He and John Crane, Ambrose O'Donell and Ambrose Hall worked outside. We didn't have electricity in the old hall and they heated the water for the tea, coffee, and dishwashing outside in four huge iron pots. Later in the day, Peter played the violin. That was the only time of the year in which my husband drank, till he got old and then he drank once in a while. This day in particular he had gotten Mat Gory to take him to Perth, and he had gotten a bottle of whisky and a case of beer for a friend. He hid the beer in a barn near the edge of the cemetery. About three in the morning Peter came in and it had started to pour rain in the meantime. He had mud everywhere. I took one look at him, and I wasn't mad but I asked him what happened. Of course, he didn't want to tell me. After a while he confessed that he had realized he had had too much to drink and laid down to have a little rest in the graveyard. He fell asleep and was awakened by the sound of a man walking away with a case of beer, which Peter thought was the case he'd hidden. He jumped up to give chase, but wasn't able to catch him, as he stumbled into an open grave. That's how he got so muddy.

"We thought no more of it at the time, but later, as stories of a ghost in the graveyard began to circulate, we knew exactly who that ghost was, but we never said as much. But that was forty or fifty years ago and we can tell the story now," Frances laughed.

The ghost of the Keenan covered bridge is still very well known in the Johnville area, even though the bridge that once spanned the Monquart was burned by vandals in May 2001. However, as in Frances's graveyard story, there is a logical explanation for at least one of the sightings, as I learned in a story shared one night by Alice Guest.

She told me, "You know the legend of the ghost of the Keenan bridge? Well, there is this little story of my dad and Earl Riley, who knew that their neighbour, Leo Hall, was coming back through the Keenan bridge after seeing his girlfriend. So they went up with two sheets into the rafters of the bridge. When they heard the horse coming they jumped to the floor with the sheets over them. The horse spooked and turned back through Kileen, through Mineral and the Pickard Road, over the Dooly Road, up the Dooly hill to Johnville. It was a big joke because Leo had to go so far around instead of a couple of miles and get the horse in and be home. And he'd seen a ghost to boot. That was one of my dad and Earl's ideas. They did a lot of tricks, I think, though I don't remember others."

One day, one of the guests in the Cullen kitchen was about to leave, and passed this blessing on to me as he took his departure. He called it the Tobique blessing: "Our father which art in heaven, please take my advice and stay there. For here on earth it's jump and strike, from four in the morning till nine at night. Amen." His conclusion was, "It was nice to meet you, Mr. Goss, take your time leaving. Please hurry back."

With stories like these, I think I'll take his advice to heart.

The Sea Monsters of Charlotte County

Any paper that serves the populace of Charlotte County, and expects fishermen to part with their hard-earned cash for a copy, has to have up-to-date news on the movement of the fish in the bay, and what is being paid for the catch in Blacks Harbour and over the line in Eastport. Occasionally, though, stranger reports of sea serpents, giant lobsters, and huge sharks have have found their way into the local papers. The few examples that follow should give you something to think about if you're about to venture out onto the Bay of Fundy.

In July 1903 there was a sea monster scare among the folks of Bayside, a village overlooking the St. Croix Estuary, and it was said that no one would venture into the St. Croix River, either to fish or to swim. For protection, several small cannons had been mounted and trained on the peaceful waters, with sharp-eyed gunners ready to hurl shells at a monster of the deep when it appeared.

This monster was not just some a figment of some tourist's imagination: it had been spotted by Walter Greenlaw, whom the *Boston Advertiser* described as "one of the best known fishermen in the village," "a total abstainer," and "an elder in the quaint little Presbyterian church on the hill."

Greenlaw reported that at the first sighting he had seen an animal with "tremendous fins [which] were kept above water and cut through with terrible swiftness. The first sets of fins were about 20 feet apart and the next set fully 50 feet behind these." After the second sighting, he reported that "the animal's head was up out of the water," but he and his brother, who was with him, were so frightened they couldn't "now even describe the conformation of the monster's head, except that the eyes were of remarkable size and as green as starboard lights."

That same month, the *St. Andrew's Beacon* of July 16 featured a similar story, telling of "a boy chased by a fish a short time ago, a boy who belongs to Bayside who was over to Robbinston on a pleasure trip. After a trip about the town he started for home, and when several hundred yards from the shore he espied two enormous fish which he described to be so immense that we dare not give them their size. Anyway, they chased him until he landed on his own native shore and then turned their heels about and went another way."

Two weeks later, on July 30, a headline in the same paper declared: "Queer Fish Drift In with the Tide." It described a "curious specimen [that had] found its way into the Howe-Quinn-Langmaid weir," and whose body was "three feet in length, two feet in depth and eight inches through the thickest part. The apology for a tail consisted of a series of scallops on the rear end of the body." The article went on to note that "just above and below the tail were two powerful fins fifteen inches in length," which "were fixed just aft of what might be termed its ears" and "laid close to the body when not in use." The eyes were described as "large and set back about six inches from a small round toothless mouth," above which there was "a hard rubbery nose." The skin was described as "dark with occasional spots and was rough and hard, like that of a dogfish," and the flesh was said to be "white as snow."

In spite of these strange reports, the *Beacon* was having nothing to do with the story of the sea monster, writing dismissively of "the *Boston Advertiser* man, who has been summering on the St. Croix [and] sends a lurid description to his paper of the appearance of the sea serpent in these waters. He must have been seeing snakes, sure enough."

But that was hardly the end of sea serpent sightings in Charlotte County. A few years later, the *St. George Granite Town Greetings* of September 11, 1907, reported that Edward Carver and Henry Gillespie were enjoying the day at Carver's cottage when they spotted a sea serpent cavorting at the buoy offshore. They rowed out for a closer look, but the creature saw them first and gave chase. They reached shore safely, concluding that the monster was a huge shark. They then got a rifle, went out again, and took a few shots at the creature. They felt confident that they had gotten him, for he made a "mighty splash" and then disappeared.

Years later, in 1930 another monster showed up in a weir off White Head island, but there was no doubt that it was a great white shark, not some unknown creature of the deep. After roping it by the tail, it was towed to a nearby cove, but not without difficulty, for at times it stopped the towboat's progress, even though the boat had a powerful motor. It eventually died, and was then measured at twelve metres, or thirty-seven feet. It yielded 210 gallons of oil. Its teeth were taken for souvenirs, and scientists who have examined the teeth today say the size of the shark was exaggerated by fishermen in the thirties. The scientists, however, were not in that weir with that shark!

In 1938, the *Evening Times Globe* of Saint John carried a story picked up from the Lank boys, fishermen on Campobello Island, who told of a monster they had encountered in 1914 off the Wolves Islands. It was grazing there on the kelp when they came upon it. Its head extended a full ten feet over the water and it was seizing grazing sheep "with lightning speed." Waiting for a chance to catch the creature, they came upon it snoozing one day, and with five men armed with axes, they proceeded to kill it. After they chopped off its head, it still writhed around for half an hour. When measured, it proved to be seventy-five feet long and had to be cut up with cross-cut saws. It took several oxen to pull the carcass to barges, where it was loaded and towed over the border to Eastport, Maine, and sold for fertilizer.

As late as 1950, reports of sea serpents were still showing up in the pages of the *Fundy Fisherman*. Prolific writer and experienced seafarer and fisherman Chester Dixon had done some investigating of numerous stories that had been told since "Pioneer days"—stories of twenty-metre water snakes, of multi-headed octopus-like creatures, of lobsters too big to pull out of the water. He did not doubt that some were true, but he did point out that such creatures were not seen as often as they once were, and that even those that were reported could often be explained as basking sharks closely following their leader as they swam just under the surface of the bay's waters.

Dixon may have been right. But even today, when whale watchers and kayakers are playfully chased by huge horse-head seals, they no doubt feel the same fright that the early pioneer fishermen did when out among the islands at the mouth of the Bay of Fundy.

The Eternal Feud of Campobello Island

When you pass through a cemetery, the study of the stones can be both interesting and mystifying. The epitaphs often contain hints of the lives of those buried there, but just as often the details of the lives of the deceased will only come clear with more study. Using the death date, it is sometimes possible to locate an obituary, which can be helpful, but just as often, there will be no record found, and no living relative, and the story of the deceased will remain obscure.

Such would have been the case with the very neat tree-surrounded Baston plot at St. Anne's Cemetery on Campobello Island, had I not become acquainted with a relative of the Bastons, one Murray

Alexander of Welshpool. Though a painful story for him to share, Murray decided it was time to do so when I came to his door on a stormy night in 2005 looking for stories about life on Campobello Island. He didn't come directly to this tale—we talked about the island's old houses, problems with crossing the border to Lubec, fishing and fishermen, and the hermit Will Calder. It was when we got to chatting about a few mutual friends from St. Anne's Church that we came to the topic of the Baston plot and its relationship to a stone that stands on the highest portion of the cemetery, on which is engraved, "Alice (Baston) Johnson, 1868–1942, Graduate Nurse."

While this is more information than many stones have, it still leaves one wondering why she included the fact that she was a graduate nurse, and why her stone is so far removed from the other Baston markers.

Firstly Murray explained that she was very proud to have been among the first, or perhaps the very first, Campobellian to have graduated from nursing school. As to her location, he said she would never have been buried with the rest of the Baston family, as she had had a falling out with some of them. He noted that her plot was not only the highest in the cemetery, but was also at one time the most decorative, surrounded as it was by carefully manicured trees and a hedge along the front nearest the roadway.

She also had trees planted around the perimeter of the Baston plot, but not for decorative purposes, Murray explained. "She had a particular axe to grind with my aunt Lena, and she hoped that the fact that the roots of the trees would spread and that the ground there had to be built up over a rocky ledge, that the combination of the two would make it impossible for my aunt to be buried there. But as you can see, it wasn't impossible. We squeezed her in," he laughed.

Murray says he can only speculate on the reason for the rift between the two, but thinks he's on fairly certain grounds about a couple of matters. As he tells it, Lena arrived on the island from England to join her mother, who had come out earlier to work as a housekeeper for a barrister, whom she eventually married. After

Murray Alexander next to the Baston grave at St. Anne's Cemetery of Campobello Island.

Lena's father had died at sea, the family had been left destitute and she had received her education at a Masonic School in England. When she came to Campobello, she became a schoolteacher and worked at several locations around the province. She met Cadwallader Baston in Welshpool, and they fell in love. While she was teaching on the Gaspé, Cadwallader built her a fine house overlooking Friar's Beach as a wedding gift. Cadwallader's sister, Alice, seemed to have been jealous of the fact that her brother had built such a nice place for his new bride, even though Alice herself lived in an equally fine house up the hill, overlooking her brother's new home.

Worse was to come, though. Murray explained, "In the house, Lena operated the public library for the island. She was devoted to the idea of getting everyone on the island reading. She spent a lot of time building the collection and seeing that it got into people's homes. In 1887 tragedy struck the family when daughter Nella chewed brimstone matches and died of poison. In Cadwallader's opinion, if Lena had not spent so much time in the library, the accident might not have happened. Alice, his sister up the hill, shared his opinion, and this led to bad blood between the two ladies."

The family then moved to Vancouver, as Cadwallader had developed some ideas for introducing lobster to the west coast, and he thought his unique way of flavouring fish might work there too. The lobster idea failed, but the fish flavouring provided him with a good income for the rest of his days. A bit of that income gave him the ability to consume more alcohol than he should have. And when he did, it loosened his tongue about the death of his daughter, and he would once again blame Lena.

Eventually, Lena left him and took their two children, Alfred and Julia, to New York. Lena worked there as a dietician, while the children went to school. Alfred began a career as a writer and correspondent for the *New York Times*, and eventually went off to China in search of a story. Some of his photos taken at the time can be seen in the Campobello Library to this day. Julia did not fare nearly as well. She was an eighteen-year-old college student enjoying life, when tragedy struck. One night, she came home from a play feeling normal and healthy, went to bed, and died in her sleep. No explanation was ever found for her death. She was brought to Campobello and buried in the Baston plot to the right of her little sister Nella.

After this, Alice had a second reason to believe that Lena was not a good mother to her children. That's when she decided to make sure the unfit mother would never be buried in the Baston plot in St. Anne's Cemetery, and thus the trees were planted, five maples and one horse chestnut.

For years the plot was looked after by Stanley Johnson, and the grounds were kept neat, with pathways laid in limestone between the sods, which were replanted every couple of years. This was done under the direction of Alice while she lived, and even after she died in 1942 the plot was neatly kept while Johnson was alive. Eventually, Cadwallader was buried there, which Murray recalls as a very difficult task. The roots had spread, the soil wasn't very deep, and Cadwallader arrived from Vancouver in a huge coffin within a tin box, which Murray says is just barely under the sods. Alfred and his wife Margaret are buried there, too, but being cremated, their ashes don't take much room.

Lena eventually moved back to the island in her last years and made it clear that she too wanted to be buried there, though she realized, as did everyone else by then, that the bodies already there had been placed in such a way that there was really no room for another one. But, as Murray noted, "We squeezed my aunt in, and she lies there to this day."

Today, Murray does his best to keep the plot neat, but he has reason to believe that perhaps Alice is not happy about the presence of Lena. He told me, "I always got along with Alice, yet, when I go to the house where she lived, I have this feeling that I am not welcome. On the other hand, I have heard that people who live there are cared for by a kindly ghost when they are sick. They feel a comfortable coolness on their forehead when they are recovering from a cold or the flu. So that could be Alice…it sounds like her, as she was known as a good nurse. But I have a strange feeling when I am there."

He continued. "When Alfred's wife, Margaret, went up to the cemetery one time to see if a stone she had made for her husband suited her, as she stood under the trees, she heard a definite voice say that she would never live on the island. She didn't like that one bit," Murray laughed.

He doesn't laugh, however, about an incident that occurred when he was working at the Baston plot one warm day. "I had done a lot of tidying up, and stood back to admire my work. I was right under the big maple on the right side of the plot. For some reason, I felt that I should move. So I did, just a couple feet to the left. Just as I did, a huge dead limb came crashing down out of that maple. Hit right where I had been standing. Now, it was a calm day, not a breath of wind. Why would it have come down right then? Why right where I was standing?"

Murray says he's left wondering if the battle between Alice and Lena is still raging despite their deaths, making it an eternal family feud. Who would've thought that such a colourful story lurked behind a simple epitaph on Campobello Island?

Miracle at Enniskillen

Like many Saint Johners who travel to Fredericton on what is called the Broad Road but is no longer broad by today's standards, I mark the halfway point from my West Saint John home to the centre of Fredericton by a fenced roadside graveyard just past the top of Petersville Hill.

I had no idea, until I did some research, that many others have also considered this a halfway point in their travels. In fact, in 1820 the government had erected a stage stop at the site, one of several between the port city and the capital city. It was a sturdy building that stood on a fieldstone base and was heated by six fireplaces.

Thirty-five years after it was built, it was taken over by Roderick O'Donnell and his wife Catherine (Collins) who maintained it as a coach stop and had a post office in one room. Catherine bore thirteen children in the period they lived in the house, 1856 to 1871. After stagecoach travel became passé, the house continued to serve as an inn, taking boarders and serving meals; in the twenties a gas bar was added and it became officially known as Halfway House.

It disappeared in 1952 as part of the takeover of the land for CFB Gagetown. Also torn down as part of that development was St. Ignatius Church, which stood at the south end of the cemetery and not far from the Halfway House. It was the fifth church that had been built by the Irish Catholics who called Enniskillen and Petersville home, the first having been erected in 1837. That first church was soon outgrown, and a larger church was built in 1863. In 1869 that structure had the misfortune of being blown down by the wind of the Saxby Gale. A temporary structure served until 1885, when a fourth church was completed on the site. It was destroyed by fire in 1933. The last church to stand on the site, and the one in which the story that follows occurred, was built under the leadership of Father Boyd in 1933–34, and despite depression conditions, was dedicated in 1940 with the twelve-thousand-dollar cost fully paid. The last mass was celebrated on June 10, 1956, by the church's first pastor, Monsignor C. T. Boyd.

Also of interest to anyone stopping at this halfway point is the memorial stone of the first resident priest of St. Ignatius, Father Luke O'Regan. It is easy to spot, as a figure of a priest is mounted atop the stone in the middle of the cemetery.

There is a very poignant story told about St. Ignatius and how it came to receive its stations of the cross. I am indebted to Linda Adams, who put together a collection of material called "Reflections of Petersville" to mark the fiftieth anniversary of the loss of Petersville, Enniskillen, and many other communities when Gagetown was built. She included in her book some stories from Eugene Campbell and Mildred McAloon, which provided the background for this piece.

She regretted that she could not contact them to thank them personally, and I must do the same.

I especially regret that I am unable to thank Mildred A. McAloon, who told the story that follows in the *New Freeman* of April 18, 1987. I found the story so touching, I feel it deserves to be shared again here:

As a native of Saint John and a nonagenarian still able (thank God) to read the Freeman, *I have been very much interested in its columns describing the upsurge of interest in those intrepid immigrants who contributed so much to the development of New Brunswick.*

But what aroused in my sister and me a feeling of elation, what has been the subject of our conversation for days, was the mention of our dearly loved grand-uncle, Bernard McAloon, in Gerry McCarthy's article "Early Irish immigrants settled Petersville-Enniskillen area" in the March 14th issue.

Uncle Barney was a Gael in the truest and noblest sense. Self educated, he was an astute, far-sighted man and an influential figure in the Petersville-Enniskillen area.

When the CPR crossed his land, it was he who persuaded the Railway to erect a station there. He had the privilege of naming it. The Railway suggested McAloon, but Bernard chose Enniskillen, the name of a lovely little town near his home in Ireland.

Bernard became Enniskillen's station master, Enniskillen's postmaster, and a successful businessman while also farming a sizeable piece of land on both sides of the track. As very young children we would clutch Uncle Barney's hand as the huge, frightening engine with its long train of freight cars roared to a stop in Enniskillen. All duties performed all papers signed, the "Monster," to our relief, purred and roared its way to Saint John or Fredericton.

But it was not as a modestly successful man in a small village that we mostly remember Uncle Barney. He was a deeply religious, prayerful man, a living saint, the recipient of a miracle, a man who predicted the day of his death, a man who, at his death merited this comment from Father Costello, CSsR, "No need to pray for your uncle. Pray to him." That we do to this day.

Eventually he was stricken with cancer of the face, leaving his whole eyeball exposed. He came to our home in Saint John where he received daily treatment by a very caring non-Catholic doctor. The doctor's orders—applying ointments, bandages, etc.—were extremely painful, but faithfully carried out by our dear mother, Rose McAloon, as constant blessings on her arose from our uncles tortured lips. After months of treatment, and extreme suffering without a word of complaint, Uncle Barney returned home to Enniskillen to die.

St. Ignatius Church needed new Stations of the Cross. In what he thought would be the last of many generous gestures to his beloved Church, he donated the fourteen. They were installed on Good Friday and offered for the dying donor. The Church was packed.

When his daughter, Annie O'Neill, returned home, her father told her the intense pain had ceased at three o'clock. She thought he was delirious, too far gone to even feel pain. But the pain did not return. Gradually the eyelids covered the eyeball, the cheek healed, and no trace of the cancer remained. He lived for seven more years.

What a joy when he visited us in Saint John, a cured man! And what a surprise to the doctor who declared "You have been cured by a power greater than mine."

The hands of chance and change forced uncle Barney to leave Enniskillen and live in Saint John with our family, which included his brother Paul, our beloved Grandfather. Paul died on January 26, 1917. Uncle Barney leaned over his coffin and said "Paul, my cup is full. I will be with you in a month's time." He died on February 26, 1917!

Our family was not destined nor did we care to blaze a trail or leave footprints on the sands of time, in any material sense. But blazoned on our escutcheon (coat of arms) are the words of our mother on that winter night 70 years ago: "A saint has died in our home. AMEN."

Thanks to Mildred A. McAloon and the other individuals named above, the history of Petersville and Enniskillen will never vanish the way their buildings have. If you find yourself driving on the Broad

Road, you will always have much to think about as you pass the site of Petersville and Enniskillen, where many years ago a miracle occurred.

Naugs and Ghosts at Harvey's Along the Line Gift Shop

Dora Boudreau of the Along the Line gift shop in Harvey has a well developed sense of humour, as will be seen in the story that follows about the naugs of the Harvey Station area. And her sense of humour might also explain why she has had more than a few ghostly experiences at her shop.

First, the naugs, which, Dora explained with a chuckle, "are friendly little fellows." You could tell there was a story to follow and it did. "When folks drop in, we're glad to tell them the story of the naugs, and if they ask, we will also tell about our ghost," she said.

Of the former, she said, "You know, in the 1960s and 70s, the naug was hunted almost to extinction in New Brunswick, but thanks to changing con-

Dora Boudreau with her collection of rare naugs—and a ghost!

ditions, naugs can be found only a country mile or so outside of Harvey itself." There she draws the line, though, and refuses to say which direction one goes or along which country mile one looks to find the naugs.

She loves to share the story of how the little fellows almost became extinct. "Back in the sixties, the young naugs, which are avocado green, and the teenage naugs, which are gold, and the mature naugs, which are various shades of brown, were sought after due to the great popularity of naugahyde as an upholstering fabric," she said with a giggle.

"Since that fashion rage passed, naugs are much more numerous," Dora told me. However, she noted that they have not recovered as quickly as scientists thought they would, because of the popularity of their eggs at Christmas. "The naug," she said, "lays a cluster of red and green eggs late in the fall, and folks around the Harvey area, which is heavily into the dairy industry, have discovered they can be gathered and used in the production of eggnog for the festive season."

Again she giggled. She giggles a lot as she has the fun of sharing this story with visitors. She also has a few unique products that they can purchase if they want to take a bit of naug lore home with them.

But she does not giggle at all when she shares the story of the ghost that lives among the naugs in the shop she runs with her husband Hugh Boudreau and craftsperson Sylvia Moorehouse. "We first became aware of an occupant of the house in 1998 when we purchased the property from Sheila Toye. During the past few years we have kept details of our experiences with the presence. My husband has seen her very clearly on several occasions and Sylvia has seen and felt her too."

Hugh described the ghost as five feet and five inches tall, and who wears dark coloured dresses and has her hair up on her head, as they did in the old days." He added, "She is quite a stately looking woman for her age."

Hugh first saw her when he had been out of the store on business, and upon returning he noted a woman standing beside the counter and talking to Dora. But when he neared the counter, there was nobody there. Hugh said, "I asked Dora who she was talking to, and she said, 'No one.' I said that there was a woman standing there and I described what she looked like, and Dora replied, 'I didn't see her.'"

However, Dora had heard stories of a ghost in the old house and at that point she called the Reverend Bill Randall who does research in the Harvey area. After she described the person, Randall said, "I'll be down in a few minutes. I'll bring you her picture." He did, and explained that the ghost was likely Minnie Glendenning, a former postmistress of the area. Dora explained that they have since received several pictures of Minnie from Bill and members of Minnie's family. The photos are all in the scrapbook that contains details of various encounters with the ghost.

They subsequently learned that Minnie Glendenning was born in 1870 and died in the thirties right in the house they now run as a craft shop. Her ghost had been seen by many of the families that lived in the house after her death. One visitor told Dora that her family would hear knocks on the doors, as well as footsteps in the hall and going up the stairs. Often they would hear water running. But when they investigated, there was never anybody in the bathroom. Sometimes they would see a shadow moving from room to room.

Dora said that she was told the mother of this family went into the bathroom to take a bath, and when she turned around, this shadowy lady was standing in the bathroom with her. According to Dora, "She was so scared that she got her husband to go up and sit in the bathroom with her while she took her bath. The couple also claimed that every night there would be a lady standing at the foot of their bed trying to pull the blankets off their bed."

Dora noted, "To this day, one of the relatives of that family refuses to come into this house. She won't even come into the gift shop and she doesn't want anything from the gift shop as she fears that the spirit may move over to her."

Sheila Toye, who owned the house before Dora and Hugh, worked in the shop doing a lot of pewter design work. Dora said, "Sometimes she would hear the front door opening and closing, and she would get up and go look, and when she got back to the table that she was working at, her work in progress would be missing. She'd retrace her steps trying to find it. When she got back to the table, there it would be there right on top of the table again. She didn't tell anybody about this until I started keeping track of the things that were happening to us. Then she told us. She also said that at night, after she would lock the building and have all the lights off she'd go out to go home and the lights inside would be back on. So she'd have to go back and make a trip through the house again. It seemed to be a playful gesture on the ghost's part. When the lights were turned out for the second time, they would stay out."

According to Dora, there is a beautiful floral fragrance associated with the ghost's appearance, which was mystifying to the Boudreaus for some time. Dora noted, "We can be out in the middle of the shop and the most delicate smell will drift by, and just as quickly it disappears. It is unbelievably beautiful. There were some ladies in from Saint John last summer. There were three of them standing talking and looking at the maple syrup products and a few other things. I have nothing in the shop that even remotely resembles this smell. I have a few spiced candles and a little bit of soap. I try to keep the smells down, as there are so many allergies now. I heard them ask one to another, 'Are you wearing perfume?' None of them was wearing any. They were picking things up and trying to find what the nice smell was. One of them came up to me and asked, 'What is that fragrance?' I said, 'I don't know, but I wish I could bottle it.'"

They have now concluded that the fragrance is associated with Minnie's death. "According to tradition, Minnie's body was found in the bathtub upstairs, and we figure she was using a very nice bath oil, or something like that, as it was very common to have a nice fragrance in your bathtub. That may also explain the many folks who have given accounts of hearing running water over the years," Dora said.

Minnie, it has been noted, is most likely to be seen, or smelled, when the train is passing through the town. "That's when she is most active," Hugh explained, adding, "the reason that most people didn't see or hear from her for years, was that the CP line almost died. Till the Irvings took it over [in 1994], you might get one train a week and on a rare week you might get two. Now there might be three or four trains per day. It always seems that after the train has gone by we'll have doors opening and the footsteps. She was the postmistress and the thought is that she is still going to the station to get the mail sack. That's our suspicion, anyway."

It's not just a family matter, either, as Sylvia Moorehouse, who works for the Boudreaus in the pewter operations, has had numerous experiences with Minnie. She said, "It's for real. I put things down and then they're gone. I ask, 'Dora, did you move that?' She says, 'I didn't touch it.' But it'll be gone."

She's also smelled the perfume which she describes "as a wonderful odour." It doesn't bother her to work in the shop alone or to come in and open up when the Boudreaus can't be there. "She's never done anything to scare me," Sylvia says of Minnie.

If things disappear too frequently, Sylvia soon takes control of the situation. "If it's something I need badly, I simply say, 'Put it back, we haven't got time,' and it comes back."

"Minnie's got a sense of humour obviously," Dora added.

In this respect, she's a lot like Dora, it would seem, and that may be why this craft shop has both naugs and ghosts to entrance unsuspecting customers.

Memorable
Moments and
Fascinating
Figures

Julia Ward Howe Brings Her Battle Hymn to Saint John

It might have all started in 1884, a leap year, when the women of Saint John got together and formed a club with the aim of bringing to the attention of the single women the names and attributes of 224 bachelors living within the city who would, in their opinion, be better off if they were married. While it may have been done for fun, it worked, and having met their objectives with at least a half-dozen men, they may have looked about for other challenges, for it was just after this that the Council of Women was formed and a number of initiatives were undertaken to further improve life in the city.

This included support for the new free library, the opening of a mission for seafarers visiting the city, agitation for a public park in the northern zone of the city, and the first push toward the establishment of playgrounds for city children, to name just a few of their successful ventures.

As their interests broadened and their influence grew, the ladies decided to bid to be hosts of the twenty-fourth Women's Congress, which would bring together women working on similar projects right across North America. Among those women was Julia Ward Howe, best known today as the writer of the beloved and still-sung "Battle Hymn of the Republic." She came to Saint John for the congress, which was held in the city in mid-September 1896, and recited her famous composition.

The *Saint John Daily Sun* reported on Thursday, September 17, 1896, that

The 24th congress of the Association for the Advancement of Women opened yesterday in the Mechanics' Institute. A private executive session was held in the morning. The afternoon session was open to the public and was largely attended. The platform was very prettily arranged. Mrs. Julia Ward Howe, the president, was in the chair, and having called the meeting to order, Mrs. Howe delivered the following address:

"The age in which we live and to which we must soon bid farewell has developed among other things two qualities which might seem to stand in irreconcilable opposition to each other. It has brought to view on the one hand a great tendency to separate of individual thought and on the other an unprecedented movement in the direction of the union which is strength...."

This is representative of the flowery and circuitous language prevalent at the time, which dominated speech after speech at the congress. As her speech continued, she noted,

This century has seen many new departures in the way of speculative thought, of practical enterprise. One of the most important of these has been the movement which has carried the thoughtful women of many communities out of the old limits, opening to them the doors of the college and leading them to many departments of public service. Among these women, Margaret Fuller stands conspicuous as an independent and resolute advocate of the true freedom and the higher culture. Florence Nightingale, Florence Tower Cobb, Elizabeth Barrett Browning, Maria Mitchell, and many others have all opened for themselves paths long untrodden by their sex.... We of this association are but a little group of women, here today and gone tomorrow. Our meeting is a very modest affair. But we come here in the name of freedom and of progress and desire to represent the great lessons which the age has taught us and which I will sum up in these words: Soundness of persuasion, liberty of pursuit, unanimity of spirit. Hoping that our three day's conference, so kindly seconded by the ladies of your council, may do something to advance these objects, I declare that the 24th congress of the Association for the Advancement of Women is open.

Later, on opening night, she responded to a speech by Mayor George Robertson—who had held up Madame La Tour (the 1645 heroine who tried to defend Fort La Tour against enemies of her husband) as an example of a heroic woman—by saying that the association appreciated the cordial welcome to Saint John, adding,

*they had long desired to come to St. John and were glad that their desires
met with such a hearty response at the hands of the St. John council. The
name St. John stood for love, peace and amity and all that was best in
our Christian religion. They looked to find these virtues eminent here. The
AAW were a band of pilgrims. When they began 24 years ago there was
hardly an association or club among women except those connected with
the churches. But the movement assumed proportions that were hardly
looked for. Wherever they went women's clubs and associations had sprung
up. They were truly thankful to God for the results which had followed their
effects. They were glad now that they had come to St. John.*

Following this speech, Harrison's Orchestra played her famous
"Battle Hymn of the Republic," but she did not recite it herself until
Friday night, following the address she had prepared for the assembly. On Thursday afternoon in the Mechanics' Institute, however,
she did recite a poem by request of those gathered. Its ten verses
were recorded in the *Sun* on Friday, September 19, but for our purposes, it is sufficient to quote only the first and last:

*There's a flag hangs over my threshold whose folds are more dear to me
Than the blood that thrills in my bosom,
it's earnest of liberty;
And dear are the stars it harbors in its sunny field of blue,
As the hope of a future heaven that lights all our dim lives through.
[...]
When the last true hearts lie bloodless,
when the fierce and false have won;
I'll press in turn to my bosom each daughter and either son,
Bid them loose the flag from its bearings and we'll lay us down to rest,
With the glory of home about us and its freedom locked in our breast.*

It's easy to see why this poem did not endure like the "Battle Hymn
of the Republic."

The next evening, that more famous poem was recited following her paper, which was titled "Women as Guardians of Social Morals." Howe began her address, which the papers noted "was an eminently clever effort," by emphasizing the timeliness of her topic: "The heart of the world was and had been heavy with expectancy. There had been heard a rumbling noise such as preceded the bursting of a volcano. The feeling was that a great European war was imminent." Her thoughts can be read in full by anyone who wishes, as they were recorded word for word in the papers of the day. At the conclusion of her effort, Harrison's orchestra again played the "Battle Hymn of the Republic" and Howe recited the lyrics for the audience.

Other events at the conference included a field trip to Red Head organized by the Natural History Society. Several of the ladies were also given the pulpits in local churches to espouse their views to a wider audience; the churches were packed to hear their comments.

At the conclusion of the event, the members of the AAW expressed their thanks to the ladies of "picturesque" Saint John, noting that they had been received with "uniform kindness and courtesy" and hoping that the congress would be a "strong link in the chain which shall bind together the hearts of women…in the common interest of educational progress." At which point, Julia Ward Howe declared the congress closed and the national anthem was sung.

The Saint John women at the conference went on to found hospitals, seafarers' missions, and public playground programs in the years to come, and they continued to champion the cause of women's rights.

The Jersey Lillie Charms New Brunswickers

One of the first rules of research is that one should stick to the subject, and not wander off in the hundreds of other interesting directions that pop up. Following this rule, I should have ignored a short

An advertisement for Lillie Langtry's performance of She Stoops to Conquer *and the renowned beauty Lillie Langtry herself.*

filler in the *Evening Times Globe* of February 13, 1929, which reported that the famous English actress Lillie Langtry, who had died the day before, had once played in Saint John in 1883. But I didn't ignore this, for I sensed an interesting story behind this passing reference. The few facts given in the filler told of two plays she had performed and a problem she had experienced claiming her jewellery from the customs inspectors. Although these facts later proved substantially incorrect, the filler did establish that she had played the port city on her 1883 tour.

Although most New Brunswickers of today know little about Lillie Langtry or her life and times, this was not the case in the 1880s, when her social life, love life, and thespian talents were covered by the Saint John daily papers on a regular basis. From their reading, residents knew that she was born Emilie LeBreton on the isle of Jersey in 1853, that she was the daughter of Rev. W. C. LeBreton, and that she had grown up in a household of boys. At twenty-one she married Edward Langtry, supposing him to be rich and able to take her into a place in the London high society that she coveted. But Edward had little money and even less desire for high society, and he kept Lillie far from the London scene.

Only after she contracted typhoid and convinced her doctor to have Edward remove her to London for her health did Lillie's life start to change. On a chance meeting with old friends, she and Edward were invited to a social evening, and the lovely Lillie immediately drew the attention of those present. She wore a simple black evening dress that became her trademark. Though her beauty was her best drawing card, Lillie complemented this God-given gift with an innate sense of knowing just what to say and how to say it, and her ability to obtain maximum value from all the social connections she made. Soon after her "discovery" by society, she was painted by the well-known Victorian artists John Everett Millais and James MacNeill Whistler. Perhaps even more important, she was celebrated in verse by the widely read and wildly popular aesthetic poet Oscar Wilde, who called her the new "Helen of Troy."

Through this social whirl, Victorian standards made her husband's presence obligatory, though he was kept very much in the background and into the liquor by most of the hosts. Eventually money simply ran out for the Langtrys. It was at this point that Lillie determined to take to the stage in order to support herself in the manner to which she had become accustomed. She was an immediate hit in her 1881 debut, *She Stoops to Conquer*. Though critics were never to admit she was a great actress, such was her reputation as a beauty that the public of England never failed to fill the theatres in which she performed. It was just two years after her London stage debut that New Brunswickers got a chance to see the Jersey Lillie and to judge for themselves whether it was beauty or talent that had led to her English stage success. Lillie chose to play the same piece in Saint John as she had when she began her career in London, *She Stoops to Conquer*.

It is quite amazing to consider that a career could be built in such a short span of time and that a reputation could cross the Atlantic so quickly in the days before the mass media and instant communications of the modern world. But Lillie Langtry was an expert in manipulation of the press. She was always available for interviews, and her romantic alliances with the Prince of Wales in England and Freddie Gebhardt in America gave reporters juicy stories to write. And these stories appeared with great regularity in papers on both sides of the Atlantic. Lillie's lifestyle led to many rumours about her conduct, but when reporters asked questions about her supposed alliances with the king or others of social importance, she simply ignored their queries if she thought them improper. Despite this, she received generally good press coverage because she had the ability to win over the scribes with her beauty, and because she was able to carry on interesting conversations on a great variety of subjects.

When Lillie came to the Maritimes, the Saint John papers were anxious to have some advance news and impressions for their readers, so they dispatched a correspondent to Bangor, Maine. Lillie had arrived in America in January of 1883 and had toured the continent for five months, generating over a quarter of a million dollars in receipts for her company. In Bangor, she was at the end of the tour, and was about to enter Canada to play Saint John and Halifax. The reporter sent from the *Daily Telegraph* noted that Lillie admitted to being tired of touring. Even so, she remained diplomatic and told the reporter that she "felt a bit happier" now that she was approaching New Brunswick. The correspondent was smitten by Lillie's loveliness, and insisted that "accounts do not exaggerate her beauty." He concluded his short interview by saying that his time with the Jersey Lillie had passed "only too quickly."

Excitement ran high in Saint John prior to Lillie's June 5 and 6 visit to the stage of the Mechanics' Institute. J. and A. MacMillan offered photos of the Jersey Lillie; the American Hair Store offered its customers Jersey Waves, Jersey Frizzes, and Langtry Hair Pins to mark the occasion; and Langtry Ice Cream was available from George Smith's stand on King Street, the name being derived because the ice cream was made from the milk of Jersey cows, which, of course, originated on the island where she had been born.

Tickets for the first night's performance of *An Unequal Match* were sold out well before the opening evening, even though their prices of $1, $1.50, and $2 were four times the regular prices of 25¢, 35¢, and 50¢. When lines formed at the Carleton Street entrance to the theatre, ushers struck for higher wages, but management promptly replaced the workers so that Saint Johners would not miss their chance to see the famous Lillie.

The audience was delighted with what it saw, and Lillie received "vociferous calls before the curtain after each act," to which "she gracefully responded," according to the *Daily Sun*. Her performance was said by the *Sun*'s scribe to be considerably better than it had been some eighteen months earlier when she first began her stage career. He went on to say that her acting was graceful, tender, womanly, and intelligent, but cautioned theatregoers that Lillie was not yet powerful enough as an actress to carry on a very dramatic role. The *Daily Telegraph*'s reviewer wrote that there did not "seem to be anything of the amateur about her appearance" and concluded, "It would be difficult for any professional to sustain the principal part of *An Unequal Match* with more dramatic tact and power than was done by Mrs. Langtry." However, the Saint John papers, like their counterparts in the rest of North America, devoted more attention to the lady herself than to her stage talents. Her beauty and dress were described in some detail.

On Wednesday afternoon, a small audience was present to witness the actress perform the part of Galatea in W. S. Gilbert's comedy *Pygmalion and Galatea*. As in most locations, Lillie was judged unequal to the role, as she "lacked the dramatic force in so trying a part," as one Saint John reporter commented. The evening performance was the play that had made her a star in London, *She Stoops to Conquer*, and the Mechanics' Institute was again filled with what the *Globe* described as a "brilliant audience." The hundred-year-old play was well known to Saint John audiences and featured Mrs. Langtry as Kate Hardcastle, a character that "suited her to perfection." As the play unwound, the audience was said to have "entered fully into the laughable situations the play presented." Lillie Langtry received frequent applause during the play and curtain calls after each of the five acts.

Following Lillie's Saint John appearance, she was off to Halifax, where she concluded her first North American tour. And though she returned to this side of the Atlantic many times, Lillie never again appeared before a Maritime audience. Her fans in this part of the world had to be content to follow her long and successful stage career and her numerous affairs of the heart through the stories that appeared regularly in the columns of their community newspapers.

Santa Claus Comes to Town, Causes Chaos

C. H. Blakeny was the owner of several businesses in Moncton, one of which was the Blakeny Hardware, where a strange incident involving Santa Claus happened when the store opened on December 11, 1936. Two days earlier, Blakeny had advertised that "Santa Claus" would appear at the store, claiming he would arrive at the Moncton airport about 5:00 and then be driven to St. George Street for 5:30. Most exciting of all, the ad declared that Santa would have free gifts for all the good boys and girls that came to see him. Now, Moncton's children were used to

This Santa promoted Blakeny's in the 1920s.

seeing Santa at Eaton's, and at the two major downtown theatres, the Capitol and the Imperial, but this appearance was going to outdo them all. Blakeny probably expected a good crowd—in fact his ad said Santa hoped to see "as many of my little friends as possible"— but he certainly did not expect the crush of children he got.

The headline in the *Moncton Daily Times* of December 12, 1936, left no doubt about what happened: "Children Swarm Streets to Give Santa Welcome: Hundreds of little ones keep police busy as St. Nick arrives in city." The story itself explained that St. Nick had broadcast a program from the store in which he read messages he had received from children listing what they wanted for Christmas. The article concluded, "Children swarmed the street in front of the store and it required the services of six of the city police to prevent accidents and to guard the children from being crushed and bruised in the jam." The *Moncton Daily Transcript* added to the story, noting that the crowd was so big it extended from the store to Highfield Street, a block away, and all traffic on St. George Street had to be detoured.

In Blakeny's history of his business life in Moncton, he mentions the incident, saying there were "thousands of kiddies awaiting the arrival of Santa" and that "children became separated from their parents, rubbers and caps were lost...one of the large plate glass windows was broken, traffic on St. George Street brought to a complete standstill." He concluded by noting the most salient fact from his point of view: "The event was a huge success and the entire stock of merchandise was sold within a few days." However, Santa never visited again; as Blakeny put it, "Because of the great congestion and danger or accidents, the show was never repeated."

Electronic Evangelizing—It's Older than You Think

It is doubtful if any of the television and radio evangelists of today realize their profession originated with the passing of a message between Halifax and Saint John on February 8, 1880. It did not occur on radio or television, but was broadcast by telephone, and St. Paul's Church in Halifax, where the message originated, claims it was the first broadcast of a church service anywhere. Besides being heard in many homes in Halifax, the broadcast was also transmitted to Saint John as part of the experiment.

Alexander Graham Bell had set the stage for such a broadcast just four years earlier when he had demonstrated the long-distance capabilities of the newly invented telephone in a one-way call between Brantford and Paris, Ontario. Later, a two-way conversation was held between Boston and Cambridgeport, which established the telephone as a viable alternative to the telegraph and mail service, at least in the minds of the experimenters and their associates.

However, the average citizen did not share the conviction of Bell and his supporters, and could not immediately see the value of the new device. The first telephone in Saint John, for instance, is believed to have been a private instrument installed by Messrs. McAvity between their King Street and Water Street establishments—basically what we would call an intercom today. By 1879, though, local exchanges were being instituted in various cities including Saint John and Halifax, but it was still a hard task to get the average person on the street to see the value of the service, and the connections

St. Paul's Church
(Anglican Church of Canada)
Halifax, N. S.

Booklet for the oldest church of British origin in Canada.

were mostly between business houses. As an example, on December 9, 1879, the Dufferin Hotel (on King Square South, where the Admiral Beatty seniors' complex now stands) was reported to have opened telephone communications with the Intercolonial Railway, the International Steamship warehouse, Worden's livery stable, and other points. The service was such a novelty that the news report carried by the *Daily Sun* congratulated the owners of the Dufferin for their "enterprise which affords so much convenience to their patrons."

In Halifax, telephone lines were being strung and connections being made in much the same manner as in Saint John. The *Morning Herald* of February 9, 1880, reported, "For sometime past, Bell's Telephone System, under the management of Mr. S. H. Smith, agent for Dominion Telegraph Co., has been in full operation in this city, a large number having been fitted up in hotels, public buildings, and business offices and private residences of our leading citizens."

It appears it was Mr. Smith's idea to arrange a broadcast from St. Paul's Church to the office of the Dominion Telegraph, and from there to Saint John. His idea may have been prompted by a desire to propagate the faith, but based on the accounts of the broadcast, it seems more likely it was the thought of commercial gain that prompted the idea.

When St. Paul's Church was connected to the telephone system on Saturday, February 7, 1880, Mr. Smith invited a number of newspaper men to the office of the Dominion Telegraph in order to hear a sermon preached from St. Paul's. Although one reporter who covered the event admitted that "newspapermen were not noted for their church attendance," they nonetheless listened attentively. They were able to report that they heard the sermon, preached ably by the Rev. G. C. Troop, as well as if they had been sitting directly in front of the pulpit at the church. The same sermon was also heard in all the homes in Halifax that had "switched on" their phones. Not only was the sermon heard, but so too were the congregational responses, the choir's singing, and the reading of the lessons. Following the service, the rector, Mrs. Troop, and friends in the congregation went to the office of the Dominion Telegraph to hear for themselves the broadcast from St. Paul's. As they listened, the strains of the organ came through the phone and they were able to report to the organist, Professor Porter, that they could hear his instrument as plainly as if they had been in the church.

Mr. Smith's demonstration of a new use for the telephone apparently impressed the reporters in attendance, as columns heralded the success of the experiment in the February 9 edition of the *Halifax Morning Chronicle*, the *Halifax Morning Herald*, and the *Saint John Daily News*. All the Halifax reporters were most positive about the broadcast, emphasizing the clarity of the words, and the potential benefit for those who were confined to their homes and might otherwise miss the Sunday services. In Saint John, however, it was reported that only the musical portion of the service was clearly audible, while the sermon and other portions of the service were not plain. Even so, the experiment was considered a success, and it was tried again at the evening service with similar results.

Thus was the concept of spreading the gospel by electrical means established. Soon after the experiment, the telephone became more and more acceptable to the public; in fact, the early 1880s proved to be a busy time for those in the telephone business. The efficient system that we enjoy today, which we'd be hard pressed to do without, dates from this period. As for broadcast evangelizing, it took a bit longer to catch on, but today it, too, is an inescapable part of the modern world.

When Jumbo Came to Town

Phineas T. Barnum dealt in superlatives. In a full page ad in the Saint John papers just prior to Dominion Day, 1885, Barnum described his show as "larger, greater, and grander than ever before." He also advertised the appearance of his latest attraction: "Jumbo, the Wonder [elephant] and children's pet," who would be making his "first and last visit to Saint John."

Barnum could never be expected to keep his word as far as a return visit was concerned. Had he been afforded the opportunity, Jumbo would have been brought back time after time, and Barnum would have suffered no loss of face in doing so. But Barnum had no opportunity to change his mind on the matter. Jumbo was killed in a railway accident less than three months after his July 6 and 7 visit to Barrack Square in the south end of the port city, and Barnum's boast of a "first and last" visit proved to be more true than even he thought.

In order to promote the circus, Barnum paraded his performers—especially Jumbo—through the streets on the day of the show to draw crowds to his spectacle.

Jumbo, who stood four metres high and weighed six tonnes, was captured as a baby in Africa and sold to the Paris Zoo, then to the London Zoo, then finally to Barnum in 1882 for ten thousand dollars. Barnum lost no time in showing off his newest attraction on arrival in New York. Jumbo was mounted in a huge wheeled cage and pulled along Broadway by sixteen horses as part of the Easter Parade of 1882. The sidewalks were jammed to witness the sight, and the next day the stands of Madison Square were packed to the rafters, just as Barnum had hoped.

Barnum followed the same successful formula to introduce Jumbo to Americans in cities and towns from coast to coast over the next three summers. According to the *Saint John Daily Telegraph*, Jumbo did not make an appearance in Canada until he came to Saint John in July 1885. The strategy of a parade followed by a performance was also used in Canada.

Jumbo's advent was announced in the three daily newspapers a week before his arrival, and at three in the morning on July 5, the sixty-car train carrying the circus arrived at the Fairville Station, on the western side of the city.

Although the train arrived in town later than expected due to a rail line breakdown, and the parade was one hour late starting, the mile-long, $1.5-million collection of acts and animals was reported to be "worth waiting for" and was described as "excelling any display ever seen in the Dominion." Jumbo, of course, was kept at the end of the parade, all the better to pique the public's interest. It worked. When the show opened there wasn't a vacant seat.

The *Daily Telegraph* summed up the circus's appearance, which drew twenty-four thousand patrons over the two days, by saying, "When Barnum was here several years ago it was thought that he had gained the acme of arenic performances. But it remained for Barnum to outdo Barnum—which he has done this time in his greatest show on earth."

After leaving Saint John, the circus appeared in Fredericton, then travelled west, eventually reaching St. Thomas, Ontario, in the second week of September. By that time there had been performances in nearly a hundred communities and the circus had travelled more than twelve thousand kilometres. The staff were getting tired as the season wound to a close, and it was their weariness that was to take the life of the star of the show.

When the circus pulled into the siding across from a field in St. Thomas, the staff pulled down a fence in order to take a shortcut across the main line of the Grand Trunk Railway. All the animals safely made their way across the line to begin the show, and the elephants Jumbo and Tom Thumb were safely led back late at night when the show ended. Jumbo, as always, was held back after the show to give the waiting children rides on his back, and was the last to leave the ring to cross the dark tracks to his waiting pen at the end of the circus train. As his trainer, Matthew Scott, led him over the tracks, the light of an unexpected and fast-moving freight train came drilling through the darkness. Jumbo made a run for safety. But the train overtook him, and after tossing Tom Thumb into the ditch, it hit Jumbo's backside, driving him headlong into a circus wagon.

Jumbo, the greatest of all elephants, the cause of jealousy to all rival showmen, the great, good natured beast, pet of children everywhere, Barnum's greatest attraction, was dead.

Even in death, Jumbo drew huge crowds. It took a hundred men to drag him off the trackbed. Barnum immediately arranged for Jumbo to be skinned and stuffed and to have his bones sent to the Smithsonian. Ever the astute businessman, Barnum charged those who gathered to witness the final chores five cents each for the privilege. Four cords of wood were required to burn the flesh left after the skinning and boning operations.

The story of the accident was carried in papers around the globe, including the Saint John dailies, which recorded the facts stated above. But Barnum dealt in superlatives, not facts. The news reports were not good enough, and a day or two later Barnum's version of the story came to light. It gave Jumbo a hero's death. This is how the *Globe* reported it:

J. A. Haigh of Barnum's show says Jumbo was killed trying to save the baby elephant Tom Thumb. As soon as Jumbo saw the train, which was only when it was close by him, he made a rush for his protege, and grasping him in his trunk, threw him away across the tracks as if he had been a kitten. The little fellow landed against a box car and lay there whining like a whipped puppy. Jumbo then tried to get out of the way himself, but it was too late, and he was crushed between the engine and the cars. He roared terribly, but his agony was short. Not only the engine, but five box cars were crowded off the track. Tom Thumb's leg was broken, and he was shot Wednesday morning.

More than a century later, people are still arguing about the incident, still trying to determine who was to blame and what happened the night Jumbo was killed. Although New Brunswickers were saddened by Jumbo's death so soon after he made his Canadian debut in the province, forty-five years later the province would be even more affected by another circus tragedy, as we will see in the next story.

The Great Circus Train Wreck

Well into the twentieth century, the arrival of a circus in New Brunswick was big news—at least as big as the Rolling Stones concert in the summer of 2005, but probably even bigger. Prior to its arrival the papers would be full of advertorials describing what those going to the circus could expect. For example, the *Moncton Daily Times* of July 21, 1930, made the following exciting promises to its readers:

Every representative of strange, wild animal life is to be found this season under the mammoth menagerie tent of the Al & G. Barnes Circus, which will give one exhibition in Moncton on Tuesday. The zoological display is estimated as being worth $1,000,000 and it is an open library of natural science from which all may read. In rebuilding and making the Al & G. Barnes circus an entirely new show, hundreds of animals were sold to zoos and parks throughout the country. In the new collection, all of which were acquired from the circus' own representatives in Africa and the Far East,

Damage from one of the worst train wrecks in the Atlantic region.

there are to be found hundreds of specimens that are new to this country and only the finest of those animals that have been seen before, but are still necessary to complete the menagerie. Everything possible is done to make the visitors to the zoological department enjoy themselves. Usually patrons are afraid to ask questions, afraid of a discourteous reply. No such fear need be felt when visiting the Al & G. Barnes Circus. In fact, there are uniformed lecturers who are paid to give information to patrons.

The "Baby Colony" is another feature of the zoological display, and this has created much interest among the youngsters. This department is fenced off to itself and it contains many tiny and amusing specimens of animals in infancy. There is no extra charge to see this exhibit which contains baby lions, tigers, pumas, elephants, camels, and many other juvenile animals. As the Al & G. Barnes Circus is known as the world's largest trained wild animal circus, many of the brutes and beasts on exhibition will later be seen going through sensational routines in the steel arena as presented by a group of subjugators of international reputation.

Above the advertorial, there was a photo of a tiger being handled by a trainer. The tiger is standing upright and the trainer appears to be placing food in his mouth. This sort of material would be carried in the papers for a week or so before the actual arrival of the circus in order to build up the interest in the community.

However, the circus of 1930 took on a whole new complexion when the train carrying the circus was involved in the most disastrous wreck ever to occur on the Canadian National Railway in the Atlantic region. The accident happened at Canaan, just outside of Moncton, two days before the circus was to open at the Moncton Race Track Grounds. Instead of announcing the arrival of the circus in Moncton, the *Times* headline screamed out, "Four people dead, and two or three others of the seventeen injured being treated in the Moncton City Hospital. May Die. While property loss is heavy."

The story went on to describe how the Al & G. Barnes circus train, consisting of twenty-nine cars en route from Newcastle to Charlottetown, had met the mishap at 6:55 AM at Canaan's Station about twenty miles west of the city of Moncton. Nine cars on the rear of the train were wrecked; three people were killed instantly and a fourth lay dying in the hospital in Moncton. It was feared that two or three others who were seriously injured might also die. The cars were badly smashed up and the track was wrecked for some distance. Animal cars on the forward part of the train were not injured. According to a statement made by an unnamed circus official, the wreck was caused by a truck arch bar failing under one of the cars.

The dead were listed as Albert Johnson of Los Angeles, California, a prop man; Frank Finnigan, also of Los Angeles, and also a prop man; J. MacFarland, believed to belong to either Toronto, Welland, or Montreal, who was a waiter; and James Arthur Stevens, a one-armed young man believed to belong to Fredericton, according to an identification card found on his person. The first three were employees of the circus, while the fourth was trespassing—in other words, taking a free ride on the rails, not an uncommon occurrence in the hungry thirties.

Among the seventeen injured and in the city hospital, all were from central Canada or the United States, save two, they being William Thibodeau of Bathurst, a prop man who had a cut on the back of the head, and Thomas Meuse of Woodstock, a canvasman who had injuries to the left foot, knee, and chest.

The story explained that nine cars behind the seventeenth car from the engine were derailed, and among them were five flat cars that were loaded with the empty cages used for the animals' street parade and circus. It was the men who were riding on these open cars who were killed. The railbed was torn up for 200 metres. On receipt of the report of the accident at railway headquarters, officials secured doctors and nurses and started a relief train to the scene of the accident. The injured were quickly conveyed to Moncton Hospital, while the dead were taken to the Tuttle Funeral Home. Once the investigation was complete, the remains of the circus train were rolled in to Moncton, rather than continuing on to Prince Edward Island, as had been the plan. Every hotel in Moncton was filled with Al & G. Barnes performers, managers, trainers, and other members of the big show, all of whom were no doubt in a state of shock.

However, they soon rallied, and it was announced that the entourage would remain a few days to repair damaged equipment and would even stage several shows. The *Times* noted,

The indomitable spirit of the circus has triumphed again. The Al & G. Barnes circus, making a wonderful recovery from a terrible catastrophe which killed four and injured 18 at Canaan Station on Sunday when the circus train left the rails on route to Moncton, gave to patrons of the great outdoor show, one of the greatest entertainments ever brought to these provinces last night at the Speedway.... It was hard to believe that a great catastrophe had befallen the circus so recently as one watched the review of the performers last evening. Thousands of Moncton citizens and others from the surrounding country attended and the big tent was well filled. There was not a hitch in the performance which featured gorgeous spectacles, skillful exhibitions of animal training, and a display of artists that has never been equaled by any circus to visit Moncton in years, if not in its history.

At one point in the presentation, the circus manager, S. Cronin, stopped the show and conveyed sincere thanks on behalf of the Al & G. Barnes circus to the citizens of Moncton, city officials, rail officials, and employees, for the "sympathy and kindness rendered to us is our hour of disaster." He continued, "When we were bleeding and dying on the railway tracks, you kind friends came to us.... I wish to take this opportunity to extend our sincere appreciation of your kindness."

Eventually, repairs were completed and the circus moved on to other Maritime locations to enchant and delight as circuses did and still do. To this day, the remains of three of those who died in the wreck are still in Moncton, and stones erected in their memory may be viewed in the Elmwood cemetery.

Ten Days in Jail, Thirty-six Lines of Verse: The Gover Murder of 1899

It seems incredible, in light of what we think we know about Victorian times, but nineteenth-century newspapers reported on murders in vivid, shocking detail. Before the matter came to the courts, every person in the community could read the evidence that the lawyers would be presenting. This happened time and time again, and the Gover Murder of 1899, as outlined in a "come-ye-all broadsheet" that would have been hollered by its writer on the streets of Fredericton, is but one example from New Brunswick's past.

The broadsheet came to my attention serendipitously while sifting through the files of the Legislative Library in Fredericton on another matter. As I can often use short and succinct descriptions of New Brunswick events when doing storytelling all over the province, and as this was a new one to me, I copied it out. After perusing the *Fredericton Daily Gleaner*'s accounts of the murder and subsequent trial, it became obvious that the statements presented by the broadsheet's author were factual and his opinions were typical of the community's reaction to the murder and trial.

The murder occurred on May 19, 1899, after a night of drinking at Alfred Gover's farm. His wife was known as one who loved her drink. Alfred himself was not one to drink, but would do so if liquor was brought to him. He was known to have a quick temper. William McLean was a frequent visitor to the Gover household. At midnight on the night of the incident, he could not make his way to his own abode, so Alfred let him stay, and the two of them slept in a room separate from Mrs. Gover. Alfred awoke at 5:00 AM and discovered that McLean was no longer in the room. Alfred thought he must have gone to the outhouse. However, he had in fact joined Mrs. Gover for a drink in her bedroom. Upon seeing them together—Mrs. Gover maintained they were not in bed, but her husband maintained they were!—Alfred went to get his gun, but he couldn't find it, so instead he got a seven-inch knife and drove it into McLean's heart. Mrs. Gover escaped out the window. Alfred gave chase, and would have killed her if a neighbour had not intervened. He gave himself up to the police and was taken to Fredericton. He never denied having killed McLean, but maintained that he had good reason to do so.

In just five weeks—an incredibly short time by today's standards—the entire matter was settled before the courts. It ended when the jury took just one hour to consider the evidence and found Alfred Gover not guilty of murder, but of the lesser charge of manslaughter.

He was sentenced to just ten days in jail.

The *Saint John Daily Sun* of June 28 contained a report from a Fredericton correspondent, who described the reaction to the trial and the sentence: "When the sentence became known throughout the city, it created a sensation. At first, it would hardly be credited, for though it was the general opinion that Gover would get off lightly, yet from two to five years in the penitentiary seemed to be the sentence that nearly everybody looked for.... On July 7th Gover will be a free man."

In the midst of this public sensation, one Fredericton scribe decided to publish the poetic broadsheet that follows. In a preamble, it was explained,

The following poem was written by request by Mr. H. G. Adams and portrays the popular feeling on this remarkable tragedy and its outcome. For the benefit of those who may not be conversant with the facts, a brief sketch of the crime is given. The scene was at Greenhill, near Fredericton, in York County. On May 26, 1899, [sic] Alfred Gover killed one [William] McLean in a fit of jealous rage. Gover was tried and sentenced to ten days in jail.

The poem followed:

Upon the left of the road at the head of Greenhill
Stands a House, that is cursed from its roof to its sill,
Where pleasures were sought by night and by day
By the youth and the aged who travelled that way.

In colour its shades are darker than night,
Yet, not darker than the one that stands on the right;
When the curse of our land was sold unto man,
'Twas the cause of that murder, deny it who can.

A soul has been summoned, accused of the crime,
That degraded a wife to the end of all time,
And severed the link by which she was bound,
God grant that mercy for her may be found.

A lawyer has fought the murderer to shield,
But there's a Judge on the Throne who the sceptre will wield,
Where no jury of twelve, empanelled will be,
And give power to that Judge a murderer to free.

The laws of our land at defiance are set,
When a man for a murder, ten days will get,
But the poor drunkard who staggers from the effects of good ale
Is politely invited to spend thirty days in our jail.

But the time will roll on and the flowers will bloom,
And McLean who was murdered will rest in his tomb,
But there's a Judge who will rule on that final day,
When the murderer and murdered must the summons obey.

That husband and wife, far advanced in their years,
Would cause the careless to tremble and melt them to tears;
As they look back on the day when at the alter they stood
And pledged themselves to each other, through evil, through good.

Their home has been shattered through the curse of drink,
Fellow travellers to eternity, stop ponder and think,
Touch not the vile monster with its venomous sting,
For your death and destruction it surely will being.

Since Gover spent so little time in jail, he may very well have heard this rhyming sermon himself as he went about his business on the streets of Fredericton.

Saint John's Cenotaph Squabble

The building of memorials to those who have died, especially in war, has long been an accepted practice. Thus, when the ladies of the Saint John IODE proposed the raising of a memorial to those who fell in World War I, and solicited proposals from noted artists, it could be assumed that they would gain immediate public support and all Saint Johners would work toward the success of such a project.

Such an assumption would be incorrect. The fact that Saint John now has a beautiful cenotaph in King's Square is taken for granted today, but for those who placed it, there was a continuous battle from the day it was first proposed in 1922 until it was finally unveiled three years later on June 10, 1925. It was not that the citizens were opposed to a suitable memorial. Far from it. At the initial meeting called to consider the matter, a good crowd turned out. Everyone in the audience addressed by Thomas H. Bullock, commissioner of harbours, ferries, and public lawns, seemed to have their own idea on what form the memorial should take. Thus, many suggestions were entertained, among them a cenotaph. But some people preferred a flagstaff and monument; others wanted a single-figure monument. Still others favoured an arch, similar to the bell tower that had graced the head of King Street prior to the Great Fire of 1877. The single point of agreement seemed to be that the memorial should stand in King's Square, preferably at the very top of King Street, a position held by the WCTU memorial fountain dedicated during Saint John's Centenary celebrations of 1883 to the memory of the Loyalist women. After much discussion, the meeting concluded with the suggestion that photos should be sought from other cities across Canada of the war memorials they had raised.

The financial response of the public was immediate, and donations began to find their way to the IODE ladies. At a second meeting held in June 1922, King's Square was designated as the site for

the memorial, and a committee was struck to negotiate a specific position in the square, the location of the WCTU fountain still being the preferred position. At a subsequent meeting in late September, it was decided to put out a national call for design proposals. In the end, forty were received, the present cenotaph being selected from the submissions in December 1922. It is the work of artist and sculptor Alfred Howell of Toronto, who described it

This cenotaph still stands in King's Square of Saint John.

to the committee as follows: "The general scheme of the design is to symbolize the triumph of victory through sacrifice and this is depicted by means of a winged bronze figure of Victory holding in her left hand a [smaller] figure of Victory, and in her right hand a cross. Standing on a globe, she thus suggests the universal victory for which men died."

The second figure on the monument was intended to portray the nation in mourning; Howell described it thusly: "At the base of the pedestal on a projecting plinth is a bronze mourning figure standing heavily draped and resting her hands on a sword. At the feet of the figure is a soldier's helmet with a spray of laurel leaves, signifying glory." Overall, the entire cenotaph would stand almost ten metres; the three-metre bronze figure of Victory itself would rest on a base of granite, and the structure would cost about twenty thousand dollars—the exact limit the local committee had set.

But it would be two-and-a-half years before Howell's work would be seen, and during those years many of the committee members working on the project must have doubted if the project would ever be finalized. While money continued to come in regularly to the committee through interested private donations, tag days, and fundraising projects, and a contract was signed with Howell, the location of the cenotaph was still an open question. Eventually, it became such a contentious issue that even a month before the cenotaph's unveiling, suggestions were still being received as to its final location.

Howell himself had understood that the memorial would be located at the head of King, described by some as the finest location for such a memorial in all of Canada. And the local committee had been working in this direction too, having obtained permission from the Women's Christian Temperance Union for the removal of their memorial fountain to another location in the square. But throughout two years of negotiations and work, not one approach had been made to the city council, and, when the committee finally appeared before council on August 24, 1924, they were refused the head-of-King location and instead referred to a location in the southwest corner of the square opposite the Admiral Beatty hotel, which was then under construction. The committee was incensed at council's decision. No location but the head of King would do, and many citizens felt locating the cenotaph elsewhere would be an injustice to those who had fallen in the Great War.

Opinions were expressed regularly in the pages of the local newspapers, and it appeared that the public was not prepared to accept council's choice of location. Neither was Alfred Howell, who insisted that his work be displayed at the head of King, as he had been led to believe it would be. But despite the outcry, council refused to change its decision, citing the heavy cost of relocating the Loyalist memorial and the future necessity of widening Charlotte Street as the basis of their decision. Public opinion against council ran so high that one writer to the editor's column suggested that if the cenotaph were located anywhere except the head of King, it should have a sign affixed to it saying, "This singular inappropriate location [was chosen] because city fathers thought it quite good enough."

About this time, it also appeared that the cenotaph contract with Howell might be in jeopardy, as it was discovered that he planned to use Upper Canadian granite in the construction of the base. However, the local committee convinced him to use a local product, Spoon Island granite, and to employ the St. George firm of Meating and Epps to fashion it. Howell apparently capitulated on the location too, and apparently long before the local populace did, for he continued to work on the figures through the winter of 1924 and 1925. When spring arrived, the monument was ready to be erected.

The location, though, was still under discussion, and Saint John's quandary was, in the opinion of some, making the city a laughing-stock. This hurried the decision-making process along, and on May 12, 1925, at a slimly attended meeting of the Cenotaph Committee, a motion was made recommending that the cenotaph be placed in King's Square in line with the Tilley Monument. The motion passed by a narrow margin, but not before a last-ditch effort by some committee members who proposed a location at the foot of King Street, in Market Square. Others had also argued that the stonework and bronze figures be placed in storage until a more suitable site could be found. Once the decision was made, the chairman of the Cenotaph Committee softened it a bit by reminding committee members that if the selected location was not found to be satisfactory, the monument could be removed at a later date for less than a thousand dollars.

Just less than a month later, on the misty evening of June 10, 1925, the cenotaph was unveiled in an impressive ceremony witnessed by some twelve thousand Saint Johners, who filled every corner of the square, perched in its trees, stretched over the WCTU Loyalist fountain, climbed on rooftops of nearby buildings, and jostled shoulder to shoulder in the streets surrounding the park. They watched as the program unfolded with solemn dignity. Massed choirs sang reverent hymns and patriotic numbers, words of prayer and praise were offered, and, finally, R. T. Hayes, MLA for the area, asked General A. H. Macdonnell to pull away the huge Union Jack that had been spread over the bronze mourning figure. This done, the guard of honour came to a sharp salute, and the Fusileers Band struck up "O Canada." Mayor Frank Potts, in accepting the cenotaph on behalf of the city, promised that council would absorb any debt still outstanding after thirty days and received a round of applause from the mist-drenched crowd.

Over the next few days, hundreds of Saint Johners visited the site of the cenotaph, many bringing sprays, wreaths, and cut flowers in memory of husbands, brothers, fathers, sons, sisters, and friends who had fallen in the Great War. After a few days, great heaps of multicoloured flowers adorned the base of the new monument. Public sentiment was strongly in favour of the finished job and the furor of the previous years quickly died, to the point that few people today suspect that any other location was ever, or could ever have been, considered for Saint John's cenotaph.

Fredericton Honours Robbie Burns (in Its Own Unique Way...)

In January 2006, just before Robbie Burns's birthday on the 25th, I wrote a column for the *Telegraph Journal* on the upcoming birthday of the bard and what it meant to people of Scottish descent. I took a straightforward approach and began by noting that each January 25, Scotsmen and Scotswomen all over the world mark the birthday of their most famous author, and that the celebration in Saint John and Fredericton are among the oldest in Canada. In fact, Saint John has been celebrating Robbie Burns's birthday since 1798.

Come have lunch under the stare of Robbie Burns on the Fredericton Green.

In 2006, New Brunswick Scots had an extra reason to celebrate, as the statue of Burns on the Green in Fredericton would be one hundred years old. Using facts gleaned from papers of the era, my column told the story of how the Burns statue came to be erected. I noted that when unveiled on October 18, 1906 (Thanksgiving Day), five thousand Scots from all over the province came to witness the ceremony. I pointed out that it was the conclusion of almost three years of work, as the idea had first been raised at a meeting of the St. Andrew's Society of Fredericton in November 1903. I also noted that the Fredericton society and neighbouring societies in Saint John, on the Miramichi, and at Restigouche had raised funds across the province to meet the $5,600 cost of the statue and granite base.

As it seemed strange to me, I included the fact that although native stone was available at both Spoon Island and St. George, the base came from Quebec granite quarries and was placed by a Toronto firm, McIntosh-Gullett. It was easier for me to understand a decision that the ten-feet-and-six-inch, 3,500-pound bronze statue of Burns himself would come from outside the province, and even outside the county, as there were no local suppliers. It also seems appropriate that an Edinburgh sculptor was chosen, namely W. Grant Stevenson.

From the news accounts, I was able to give a bit of background on the site, and noted that as the day approached for the unveiling, much work was still needed to neaten up the grounds. Accounts of the day noted that for years the area had numerous finger wharves, served as a transfer point for lumber, and was sometimes a pasture for cows. Mayor Fenety's attempts to plant trees and seed the ground, in 1877 and again in 1887, did not produce lasting results. As late as 1901, Fredericton's city council was struggling to close garbage dumps in the area. Eventually they succeeded, and today the Fredericton Green stretches along the River St. John, studded with huge trees that provide great shadowy places to enjoy lunch and watch as joggers, bikers, and walkers enjoy the best riverside pathways in the province. And, of course, there are also the many statues and other works of art that are found in and around the Green, including that of Burns.

Now, normally, a column like this does not elicit much response, but this one generated three separate comments over the next few months that added to the information I had presented.

First, I was told that the Green was not the first location chosen for the statue; originally, the St. Andrew's Society received permission to erect a statue on the lawn of the Anglican Cathedral just west of the present location. However, upon learning that the figure would be of Burns, and knowing of his propensity for drink, the Anglicans changed their mind.

Based on the second and third comments that came my way, perhaps the churchmen did the right thing. Though news accounts make no mention of it, I was told that when Burns was unveiled, some wags had painted his nose red and had placed a whiskey bottle under his arm. Keeping that dubious tradition alive, frosh week activities at the University of New Brunswick have been known to trickle down the hill to the Green; not only has Burns had bottles about his feet, but from time to time phallic symbols have been placed on his person.

So the response to my column has resulted in a more rounded story about this cherished Fredericton landmark, and that's as it should be. Certainly anyone who could write a poem to a wee mouse would see the humour in these acts—even if those responsible for the erection and upkeep of the statue might not.

Alex Haley Sails into Dalhousie

It probably will come as some surprise to most readers of this book to learn that Alex Haley, famed author of *Roots*, visited Dalhousie on at least two occasions. It certainly was a surprise to wharfinger Beezie Sullivan when she first encountered the famed author. It happened in August of 1988 when she went to call on the captain of the cast vessel *Husky*.

"I was appointed as the only female wharfinger in Canada, and when ships came into Dalhousie, I was responsible for seeing that they treated government property properly when tied up at the public wharf," Beezie told me when I visited her in her hometown. Though she is now retired from that role, she remembers clearly the day that Alex Haley showed up on a ship that was loading paper for overseas markets from the huge mill that drives the town's economy.

"It was customary for me to visit the captain on the vessel, just to see if there was anything he needed while in port. On this occasion, while we were talking, a rap came on his door, and in stepped

Alex Haley. 'I wonder if I could get a typewriter fixed while we're docked,' he said to the captain. 'I know you!' I said to Mr. Haley, and introduced myself. The captain said, 'If anyone can find someone to fix your typewriter, Beezie can,' and I went with Mr. Haley to see the typewriter. It was an old-fashioned one, but I knew a man in Campbellton who could probably do the job. I called Mr. Englehart, told him the situation and he offered to come right down to the ship and see what he could do. He fixed it and never even charged Mr. Haley," she laughed.

It was to be the first of many kindnesses the author was to receive on his short stay in the community, and he was so impressed with the area and its people that he came back the following year on another vessel for a second helping of their friendliness.

Beezie explained, "As I understand it, Haley served on the navy in the Second World War, I think as a cook, but I am not sure of that. When he became famous [after *Roots*], he just could not get away from the press, from people who wanted him to speak, could not even walk down the street without recognition. So he would get on an ocean-going vessel, along with his secretary George Simms, so he could have solitude and write."

Perhaps due to the kindness displayed in the repair of his typewriter, Haley readily

*Doreen MacLean (left) and author
Alex Haley (right).*

agreed to a tour of the Dalhousie area when Beezie proposed it. Of course, any tour must include the mayor of the town, and that is where Sandy MacLean comes into the story. As Sandy recalls it, "When Beezie brought him around to the town hall, I joined the tour she had planned and we drove Mr. Haley all over the area. We took him down to the Eel River Reserve, out to the Charlo Airport, we went to the museum and the library, showed him the schools, and took him to the Farmer's Market. Everywhere we went, people recognized him, and people rushed off to bring copies of *Roots* for him to sign. He was most accommodating."

Beezie picked up the story from there, noting that in a few short hours, Haley signed books printed in English, French, Swedish, and German. "He was surprised by this and told us the diversity of our small town was amazing. He said he was working on a book about a small town and that what he was experiencing in Dalhousie would be part of the story," she noted.

He had some new food experiences while in the area, too, enjoying lobster and salmon. "When he said he had never seen a whole salmon," Beezie recalled, "one of our residents dug into his freezer and gave him one, which he took back to the ship." He also took a bag of goodies that Sandy's wife, Doreen, prepared for him after a visit to their Adelaide Street home for a meal.

Once back on the ship, Mr. Haley wrote,

Alex Haley,
Norris, Tennessee, 37828
MV Cast Husky
Dalhousie to Antwerp
August 21 1988

Dear Sandy and Doreen,
Sandy will recall that visiting the airport, I used the chance to telephone my wife what a marvelous and unexpected pleasure I'd experienced in a town of which I'd never heard called "Dalhousie." When I play it back in

my mind, George and I really were given the red carpet treatment, essen-tially between yourselves and Beezie. I want now to express to you directly that this past two days will stick with me as much more than some average passing memory. You are—all whom I met, and George shares this same feeling—such unusual and warmly hospitable and generous people! (Right now I am looking at my two jars of preserves!) I truly do look forward to returning next year on the Maria Gorthon, and I will think of your family (including two stray dogs and killer cat) many times before then.

Alex
FIND THE GOOD—AND PRAISE IT

And he did indeed return for another round of Dalhousie hospi-tality—a kind of hospitality that is not reserved just for the famous, but available to anyone who takes the time to visit this Bay of Chaleur community.

Clippings and
Conversations

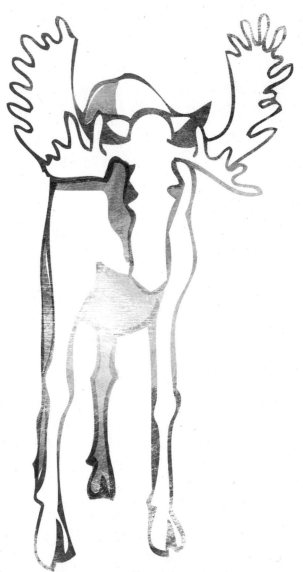

Scrapbooking is big these days, but many scrapbookers would be surprised to know that it is not a new idea, just a new way of doing something our ancestors enjoyed. Were it not for scrapbooks kept by men and women of the past, many of the stories that appear in this book would not have been included, for often my first glimpse of a story is through a clipping in a yellowing scrapbook that someone lovingly kept. Many of these are very brittle, but I am always glad to have the opportunity to flip through them. In other cases, I am able to view scrapbooks kept by people like W. O. Raymond, Clarence Ward, William F. Ganong, David Russell Jack, or John Willet because they were turned over to a library or museum, and then microfilmed so that one never need worry again about how brittle they will get.

In a way, I view the collections of the Legislative Library, the Provincial Archives, the New Brunswick Museum, local museums, and especially the Saint John Regional Library as one giant scrapbook, containing hundreds of interesting stories that might be lost if they had not been fixed in a scrapbook or filed away. And then there is the "oral scrapbook" of stories that have been remembered and passed down by amateur storytellers. What follows are some of the shorter stories that have caught my eye, or ear, and which shed light on things that those who went before us considered interesting, amusing, or just plain odd.

Dropped Booze on Main Street

A clipping from the *Moncton Daily Times*, December 26, 1912:

Late Christmas Eve *a gentleman, accompanied by a lady, and carrying a neatly wrapped parcel under his arm was observed coming down Main Street. He appeared to be a stranger and when he was right in front of Mr. H. L. Bass' store, he chanced to collide with a passing pedestrian with the result that his parcel fell to the ground with the loud crash of breaking bottles. Instantly, the powerful odor of booze rose from the wreck and was wafted down the street on the strong breeze which was blowing causing citizens to sniff the atmosphere with suspicious nostrils. The stranger, evidently fearing that the criminal scent should reach the noses of the police officers, hastily seized his companion by the hand and beat it out of reach before a move could be made to learn his identity.*

Main Street, Moncton, N.B.—10

Early postcard of Moncton showing Main Street—the scene of the crime!

A Very Hungry Fish

On May 26, 1938, the "Man on the Street" column of the *Evening Times Globe*, written by Ian Sclanders, later editor of *Macleans*, was devoted to fish stories, as the season had just opened on the 24th of May weekend. Sclanders's first story was based on a Canadian Press report from Portuguese Cove, Nova Scotia:

"A sickly looking codfish, pulled from the depths of the Atlantic, yielded George Sadler, merchant, a pair of socks.

"When Sadler opened the 15 pound cod he found a pair of socks neatly folded. The socks were almost new."

Mr. Sparks, as he read the item, remarked to himself that most people wouldn't believe it, even if it was true. But he himself wasn't one of the doubters.

For he knew that just last spring, at Beaver Harbour, a handful of miles from Saint John, George Bates caught a codfish which contained one sock. In the sock was a hard object, presumed by Mr. Bates, when he first felt it, to be a man's foot. On investigation it turned out to be a monkey wrench, for which the sock had been used as a container, and which, evidently, had been dropped overboard from some ship.

Captain Oscar Outhouse of Beaver Harbour, Mr. Sparks relates, says that cod caught before a storm frequently are full of stones which they consume as ballast when the undertow starts kicking up, and that as many as seven stones as big as a man's fist have been found in one large cod.

Mr. Sparks has also heard the saying of fishermen that cod are the retrievers of the deep and that if you drop overboard an object that is possible for them to swallow, such as a knife or a wrench or

a mitten, to just keep on fishing and eventually you'll get it back—
if somebody else doesn't first catch the fish which consumed your
property.

He quotes Captain Walter Wadlyn, a grand "old salt," as his
authority for the fact that there is a fishing bank out of Gloucester
where the cod caught have nothing in their stomachs but fresh water.
They go to this particular bank in large schools, according to the
tale, to drink from the springs of fresh water which bubble from it
with such force that 'fountains' of fresh water are formed.

A Very Thirsty Fish

A clipping from the *Fundy Fisherman* of July 24, 1930, about a "Cod
Caught Carrying Contraband":

Deer Island, July 21—Swallowing a half-pint of liquor without removing the cork—Well, it sounds like a Houdini feat, but the trick was
turned sometime recently by a pompous looking codfish, an inhabit-
ant of the Grand Manan Banks, according to James Dagget of the
life saving station at Seal Cove.

Mr. Dagget said that the fish was landed by two fishermen at
Walter Benson's fish stand at White Head, and the half-pint flask of
liquor removed from the fish's stomach, intact.

It may be that the cod carried the liquor in case of emergency,
such as seasickness, cod-headaches, etc. Evidently, the particular fish
referred to did not believe in boozing while at sea, or the cork would
have been removed. It has been suggested that the Bay of Fundy
codfish have caught on to the rum-running racket, and that they are
carrying liquor to points along the US coast.

The Fish Weren't Biting...but Something Else Was

A clipping from the *Saint John Daily Sun*, July 10, 1903:

Matapedia, Canada—July 8. What fishermen come hither for is, of course, to catch salmon. But there are times when the great silver fellows sulk behind the sheltering rocks at the bottom of the swift current and disdain to rise to any lure, however carefully chosen and cunningly cast. At time like these, one seeks consolation in the stories of the guides, for if the Restigouche River region is famous for the largest salmon in the world, so too do the Restigouche canoemen bear an equally well-deserved fame for the largest fish stories known to the disciples of Izaak Walton. For instance, there is Archie MacDougal's story of the long cast.

Archie is an old-timer, one of the most skillful of bowmen—and the bowman is captain and master of the canoe—and well versed in all the arts of salmonry.

"Mind you," says Archie, "it is not the largest cast I ever made. I'm not saying that at all. Not by any means. But, considering the circumstances, I'll hold by it to beat any thrown out in these waters.

"I was fishing with Mr. Davies. You mind Davies, the great tobacco man? A gale was blowing from the west and we'd had spare luck.

"Just after we'd taken a long drop and anchored in a likely pool we saw a great fellow rise upstream of our anchor. It might have been a hundred and ten feet from the bow. Now, you'll mind that a salmon, when he rises, goes down in the same spot and stays there.

"Mr. Davies cast for the spot, but the wind being so heavy against him he couldn't reach it. No shame to him, for he threw a good line.

"'If we anchor, Archie,' says he, 'we may disturb him. Do you think you could drop a fly over his nose?'

"'I'll try it,' says I. 'He's a thirty pounder, for sure.'

Restigouche Sam—the second-biggest fighter of the rivers that run into the Bay of Chaleur.

"My first cast fell short. The gale tangled up my second attempt and Mr. Davies smiled. That stirred me up. I shook out the line, got myself a handful of slack from the reel and put all the whip of the rod—and a pretty bit of green heart she was—into the finest cast of my record. As the fly took up the slack I knew I was over the spot and well beyond it. One hundred feet that throw must have been measured. The spot where the salmon had landed was a little scoop in the bank. In the calm of the water there the fly landed.

"Then what do you think happened. Well sir, didn't a beaver take it! Right out from under the bank he came—and thump, he had the hook, then the trouble began. The biggest salmon ever spawned never had half the fight of that reptile. Out into the river he went with a rush and the old reel singing a song of disaster and smoking like a new pipe, with the friction.

"'Cut the anchor rope!' I yelled to Mr. Davies. And his knife was through it in a second. Dollar and a half that anchor cost me.

"Down the stream we went, eight mile an hour with the current, and across the stream, ten miles an hour with the berth. Every half minute or so he'd come up out of the water, and then his big fat tail would whop the surface like a revolver-shot and the water would part fifty feet. After he'd turned a few dozen of these hand-springs, he set off downstream, and the fight was on in earnest.

"'If we can get to shore below him and coax him in,' said Mr. Davies, very much excited, 'I'll get out and gaff him.'

"'You stay in the canoe,' says I, 'unless you've got a leg to spare. That fellow'd lop it off like a twig if he caught you in the water. We'll just have to tire him out and drown him.'

"Well, sir, if that beaver didn't tow us down the river, through the rapids, and around the islands for nigh on two hours I hope I may never prick another salmon. We might have been following him yet if we hadn't met another canoe with a man in it that had a revolver. I handed the rod to Mr. Davies, and the beaver bear hauled him out of the boat, for he wasn't used to such pulling. Finally he coaxed the reptile to the surface and I loaded old paddle tail up with lead. When we had him safe ashore Mr. Davies turned to me with a long sigh and says he: 'Archie, salmon fishing isn't much. Let's only fish for beaver after this.'"

William Ganong's New Brunswick Scrapbook

William Ganong (1864–1941) was a noted botanist and historian. Born and raised in Saint John, he spent his career as a professor at Smith College in Northampton, Massachusetts. Throughout his life, he compiled scrapbooks of clippings about New Brunswick news, some of which are now in the collection of the New Brunswick Museum. The following are clippings from those scrapbooks.

#1

Game of all kinds swarmed in the forests and streams. When this land was first settled, moose, deer, and bear were numerous, but the moose was the most hunted on account of the superior quality of its flesh. A rather remarkable story is told of an old settler who determined one very cold day in the month of January to go on a moose hunt. So slipping on his snowshoes, and throwing his musket across his shoulders, he trudged off into the forest. In the course of the day he shot a fine animal which he skinned and quartered, and after placing it upon his back, started for home. The night soon overtook him, and as it rapidly grew very dark, he quickly realized that to proceed would be unwise, as he might lose his way and that to remain where he was would be equally dangerous as the night was extremely cold, and he might freeze to death. Suddenly a bright idea struck him and he quickly acted upon it. Taking the moose hide off his back, he spread it out upon the snow, then lying upon his back at the extreme edge of the hide, he rolled over and over while holding on to the edge of the skin at the same time. Thus he became literally enveloped in moose hide. Then after seeking a most secluded nook...he turned in for the night. Imagine his surprise in the morning when he found himself a prisoner. The moose hide had frozen during the night and he found it impossible to extradite himself. In this condition he in some manner made his way home, little the worse for the night out.

#2

In the 1860s wolves were still a big problem in the Havelock area, and settlers were determined, if possible, to rid themselves of these animals. They accordingly armed themselves with guns, clubs, etc. and started out on what became known as the great wolf chase. They went through the woods in a long column placed in a position that each hunter could distinguish his right and left hand man. Thus every living creature was driven before them and the settlers were not again troubled with wolves.

The Havelock Cemetery, about a quarter mile from the corner, is beautifully shaped and neatly laid out. On a tasteful monument standing near the entrance is the following: In loving memory of Captain Benjamin D. Fownes, who died at Okin Islands, China Sea, September 22, 1890. Captain Fownes was in Command of the Saint John ship *Lizzie Troop*, and was accompanied on the voyage by his wife and child. Two days after leaving Nagasaki, Japan, for Portland,

Oregon, the vessel was driven ashore in a storm and dashed to pieces. Captain and Mrs. Fownes were dragged to land by the natives, but the captain's back was broken and he died in great agony. Their child was never seen after the ship struck.

3

From the *Saint Andrew's Beacon*, February 4, 1892:
When the Honourable Charles Connell of Woodstock was Postmaster General of New Brunswick, he issued a stamp with his own head instead of the Queen. A great course of ridicule and indignation greeted the stamp, and it was recalled and destroyed. If Connell had saved a big lot of them, they would be worth more now if put on the market cautiously, than the large estate he left to his heirs. At a recent auction of postage stamps in London, a Connell stamp, though slightly damaged, was knocked down for 16 pounds, ten shillings, about $82. The sale was conducted by Messrs. Cleveley Wilson and Company, 63 Chancery Lane. Mr. Connell's face and name will be handed down the ages and be familiar when those of Gladstone are forgotten by reason of his stamp issue. Such is fame from the world.

#4

From the *St. Croix Courier*, July 16, 1903:
The haunted camp seemed to hold its own as far as supernatural manifestations are concerned. For a certain resident, who by the way is a devout believer in divining rods, told your correspondent a marvellous tale regarding the happenings when he made a visit to the camps some nights ago. Seems some of the parties concerned induced him to go there with his divining rod and try to locate the treasure presumed to have been buried by Kidd or Teach or others of the nautical confraternity of rascals whose name is legion. His experience with lights and noises and paralytic shock is something altogether too graphic for my pen to record. How much is imagina-

tion, one cannot tell but none dare doubt the veracity of the story as told by the diviner who has unbounded faith in the mysterious.

#5

From the *St. Croix Courier*, July 9, 1903:
A strange occurrence is reported from the harbour. One of the fishing camps is said to be haunted. The occupants state that on several nights about eleven or twelve o'clock, they complain that they hear a boat row ashore below the camp, then footsteps approach and heavy blows are dealt to the door. On investigation by the inmates, nothing unusual is to be seen. But some of them are so uneasy that they have shifted their quarters and refuse to sleep at the camp. Various theories are suggested by the fishermen such as Captain Kidd, old man Salkeld, etc.

A Lively Corpse

A clipping from the *Granite Town Greeting*, June 7, 1912:

A country doctor returning from a visit in the small hours of the morning, in the days when there were "body snatchers," had to pass a secluded burial ground in which a deceased patient had been interred the day before. He saw a horse and trap unattended

The author shares a ghostly story on a cemetery walk in Saint John.

on the roadside. Looking cautiously over the wall, he saw that two men had just disinterred the corpse and placed it in a sitting position on the seat of the trap, wrapped in a dark cloak, so that when they drove away the body would look like a third man, sitting between the other two. In the meantime, they then got over the wall again to fill in the grave. The doctor lifted the corpse down from the trap, laid it under the wall, and seated himself in its place. After a short time the two men got over the wall again, threw their spades into the back of the trap, seated themselves one on each side of the cloaked doctor, and drove off. Presently one of the men said to the other: "The body seems to be warm still." The other replied: "So it is." Then the supposed corpse said: "Warm! If you had been where I have been for the last twenty-four hours you would be warm too!" The two men leaped with a yell out of the trap at opposite sides and ran for their lives.

Captain Dow's Donuts

A clipping from the vertical file of the Campobello Library:

On Campobello Island, they like to tell a story about Captain Dow, an old time sea captain who sailed mostly along the Maine coast but ventured up into the Bay of Fundy and New Brunswick from time to time. His favourite snack was donuts, which the cook would prepare by throwing dough into the boiling fat. They were very good donuts, but they were very heavy in the belly—so heavy, in fact, that anyone who ate too many and fell overboard would be sure to drown. The sailors were willing to overlook that potential hazard because the donuts were so good.

One night, the captain was on a trip from Portland to Saint John when a raging storm blew up the east coast. He had spent the whole evening at the wheel and he got mighty hungry. He could think about nothing but donuts. He wanted to call the cook to make some, but knew that if the boat went down he would go straight to the bottom with the heavy donuts in his belly.

However, after many hours he got so hungry that he gave in and called for donuts and coffee to be served. His men decided to join him. As they ate, the storm worsened. The captain had to return to the wheel but he was still hungry, so he took a dozen donuts with him. In order to hold onto the donuts, he poked them onto the spokes of the helm. Whenever he got hungry, he pulled one off and enjoyed his snack. This was the first time donuts ever had holes punched in their middles.

Such an idea might never have caught on, except that the storm got so bad that the boat sank. Captain Dow's crew went straight to the bottom, as they had all eaten the heavy donuts without holes. The captain, though, remained afloat because his donuts had been lighter. He was able to rescue his men and get them ashore. Ever after, he decreed that all donuts on his vessels must have holes punched in them by the cook before they were delivered to the men. The idea spread from ship to ship, and most donuts you see today do indeed have holes—except at Tim's, but seeing as there's no Tim's on Campobello, the story is still a good one there.

Findings of the Historical Society

The following story, headlined "Another Utopia Stone," appeared in the *Daily Sun* on November 1, 1894:

The regular monthly meeting of the N.B. Historical Society took place last evening. A large number of communications were read and several donations from sister societies were reported. H. H. Pickett was elected to membership.

J. Vroom of St. Stephen, a corresponding member of the society, sent the following communication:

"At Hill's Point, St. David, the peninsula lying between Waweig and Oak Bay, where there are some interesting old French cellars, there is also a curious stone, to which my attention was called a few days ago by Thos. Hill, the owner of the place. It is a boulder of red granite, about eight feet in diameter, bearing the marks of metal tools.

"The stone rests on the top of a ledge of the native rock. Originally nearly spherical in shape, it has been split through at about one third of the diameter, leaving a fairly smooth vertical face. The segment taken off lies at the foot of the ledge, broken in two or three pieces. The face exposed by the loss of this segment is much weathered, being hardly distinguishable in this respect from the convex surface of the boulder.

"Twelve or 15 inches from the edge of the vertical face is a line of drill holes connected by hammer marks, which runs up over the top and down on the opposite side until it nearly encircles the boulder. The intention of the workmen seems to have been to cut out of the stone a large disc, which would be eight feet across and a foot or more in thickness; but apparently when one side had been split off either the cleavage or the quality of the stone proved unsatisfactory, and the work was therefore abandoned. But, strangely to say, there are no drill holes or other discernible marks of tools about the broken face.

"The stone stands in an exposed place, near the edge of an open field that has been in cultivation for perhaps a century. No one knows who did the cutting, and it is therefore supposed to be the work of the French settlers. It does not seem to me, however, that either the French inhabitants or the early English would have wanted a millstone of such dimensions, and I cannot imagine any other probable use they would have for it. Could it have been the work of the supposed prehistoric people who carved out of the same material the remarkable Lake Utopia stone now preserved in the rooms of the Natural History Society?"

A Supposed Murder in Milltown

A clipping from the *St. Croix Courier*, June 16, 1870:

One Mr. Tapley, who, upon passing through a lonely and remote portion of the Easton estate field at Middle Landing, noticed that the earth was turned up in just one spot. He examined the area closely, and came to the conclusion that someone had recently been buried there. Upon arriving in town, he soon had the ears of many of the leading citizens, and the next day a large number of them joined him on a journey to the site of the grave. Many carried picks and shovels in order to unearth the remains of the victim of the foul deed that Tapley was certain had occurred. And remains were indeed found— but they were those of a cow, not a human. The cow had belonged to John S. Hutchings and had died some months earlier, at which point its owner had disposed of it in the Easton field.

Treed by a Bull Moose

The *Moncton Times* of December 19, 1904, picked up a story from the *Fredericton Gleaner* about a well-known sport in the province, one Charlie Cremins, and his misadventure with a bull moose. As Charlie told the story, he said he was running a line for a lumbering concern near his hunting camps on the Nepisiquit River when he came across a moose yard in which there were eleven animals, six of them being bull moose. In all his years of hunting, he had never seen so many moose together except in a winter yard. All had huge antlers of at least eleven inches, and one had antlers that spread five feet across, according to Charlie.

He decided to have some fun, so he crept up on the beasts, and when one of the big bulls grunted, he grunted back. This agitated

It's not wise to grunt at a moose unless it's this one in Market Square.

the moose, which began to show unwelcome interest in Charlie. Charlie showed him his heels and ran toward a thicket for protection. In the middle of the thicket, he spotted a big tree, which he climbed. This didn't escape the moose's notice, and he made for the tree. The moose had such a reach with his antlers that he knocked Charlie's only weapon, an axe, out of his hands. For a time, Charlie was convinced there would be one less guide in the woods once the moose was through with him, but after four hours, the moose decided he'd had enough sport with the sport and ambled off to rejoin his herd. Charlie climbed down and made the seven miles back to his camp in record time, looking behind him all the way, lest the moose was giving chase. As a result of the experience, he resolved never to grunt at big moose again—unless he was carrying a rifle.

Swapping Stories on the Rails

Cecil Steeves and Harold Lewis both worked for CN in Moncton, and from time to time they would swap stories. Cecil told me these two about his lifelong pal and co-worker.

One day, Harold Lewis was downtown shopping with his wife and daughter. Both he and his wife had shopping bags full of parcels. His wife wore a dark red coat. They parted to allow her to do some more shopping. His little girl, who had stayed with him, decided she wanted to carry a parcel just like her mother. Harold said, "I'll get one out of your mother's bag," and looked around for his wife. He spotted a lady wearing a dark red coat, went over to her, and dug his hand down into her shopping bag to get a small parcel.

A strange woman looked at him with astonishment and said, "What's up Jack?"

Believe it or not, the street under this subway was once coated with molasses!

Harold looked up into her face and saw that it was not his wife at all! He tried to explain that his wife had a coat like hers and said, "Wait till I find her for you." The woman just looked at him and never said a word. After a lot of explanation and what seemed like an eternity, his wife came along and cleared up the mess.

She later told Harold, "I wonder what would have happened if I had said, 'I've never seen this man before in my life'?"

On another occasion, earlier in life, Harold mowed the lawn and then went downtown on his bicycle. A truck had lost a puncheon of molasses on the subway hill and it broke open and coated the street under the subway. Harold came along on his bicycle and, thinking the molasses was mud, gave some extra hard pushes to get through without splashing too much. When he hit the molasses, the bicycle stopped—but he didn't! He flew off and got plastered with the molasses. He picked himself up and wheeled his bike home. When he got to the house, he walked across the lawn that he had just mowed, and the freshly cut grass stuck all over his molasses-covered body. When he got into the house he gave his mother an awful scare—she thought he looked like a "little green man from Mars"!

A Tour of the Old Fredericton Gaol

The *Fredericton Capital* of January 22, 1887, contained the following description of conditions at the county jail of the day, which revealed quite a variance in the quality of the accommodations and brought to life one prisoner's particular skill with his knife:

On Tuesday afternoon the County Council paid a visit of inspection to the County Gaol where they were hospitably received by the Deputy Sheriff. After entering the gloomy portals of this Tartarean stronghold, those of the councillors who had not before visited it were agreeably surprised to find the first and second stories laid off in comfortable rooms of some twelve feet square, or more, and provided with elegant iron bedsteads. Some of these rooms were heated by hot air from the furnace, and others by old fashioned box stove.

The rooms on the second storey, but for the iron bars ominously checkering the windows, were undistinguished from those of an ordinary dwelling. On this flat was shown the bathroom provided with hot and cold water, and it excited the envy of many of the visitors, whose residence is without this modern improvement.

Although the building begins to show the signs of age, and though the walls of the prisoners' rooms would be better off with a coat or two of whitewash just to destroy the animaux, as it were, the whole of the interior was scrupulously fresh and clean. The introduction of water from the mains has greatly improved the sanitary conditions of the gaol, and provided a ready means of extinguishing an incipient fire.

After inspecting the upper regions, Mr. Hawthorne led the way to the dungeons in the basement where refractory prisoners are placed until they unconditionally submit to the rules of the institution. Those cells are built of solid stone and are constructed on the principal of a wine cellar, with no apparent means of ventilation but the door, and this, when shut, excludes both air and light. One of the councillors went bravely in and had the doors closed on him, but in a few moments satisfied his curiosity. As there is no artificial heat in this part of the gaol, the condition of a prisoner in these cells, in such weather as this, would be a shade worse than that of the prisoner of Chillon. But no one need be placed there except as a result of his own misconduct.

In one of the rooms on the first story, the prisoner Brownell, who was prosecuted by the New Brunswick Railway Co. for taking an unlawful ride on one of their lorries, was confined. He is evidently handy with graving tools, for on the floor of his room he has very neatly carved the following "memoriam" in the form of a grave stone:

IN

MEMORY

OF

J. BROWNELL

WHO LAID FIFTY DAYS

FOR

THE ACCOMMODATION

OF THE

NEW BRUNSWICK RAILWAY CO.

BLEST ARE THEY WHO

CAN LIE IN PEACE

The letters are all Roman Capitals and are well cut.

Brownell has also been serving out a term for violation of the Scott Act [i.e., Prohibition] and has turned his knowledge of the interior economy of flasks to some account. The councillors were shown a pint flask that had of yore been filled with usquebaugh, anglice [Scotch whisky], but is now occupied by a miniature lumber sled, complete in every respect. It fills the entire cavity of the flask, and is supplied with pail, axe, chains, cant-dogs, peavies and hand spikes. His little knife was all that Brownell required to use on the piece of kindling wood of which this curiosity was manufactured. The man who can exhibit such ingenuity as this model displays is worth of a higher niche in the temple of fame than is to be found in Hawthorne's Hotel.

After making a thorough inspection of the building and the yard and noting what repairs were required, the councillors retired quite satisfied that the Deputy Sheriff is doing the best he can to conduct the affairs of the gaol with due regard to humanity and the security of the prisoners.

The Other Dungarvon Whooper

It was while on a visit to Cecil Steeves that I learned that there are at least two Dungarvon Whoopers. Most folks know the oft-told tale of the poor cook murdered by the camp boss, who then stole the little purse of money he had on his person. Buried just outside the lumber camp, he's a restless ghost whose blood-curdling whoop has been heard in the Miramichi woodlands ever since. The whoops were similar to those emitted by the steam locomotives that ran down the valley, so the train became known as the Dungarvon Whooper. Cecil shared this poem he collected while working for the CN in Moncton:

Here comes the Whooper, so listen to her wail
She's a steam locomotive with the devil in her tail.
I've heard all about her, but why does she scream?
She thinks she's an old ghost from Dungarvon Stream.
Blackville girls and Doaktown, she's moving fast and free
And she sets the rails a-ringing through the Valley Miramichi.

She came down to Newcastle from old Quarryville
Smoking up the slope and she'd whistle loud and shrill.
She was haulin' shorty boys from Dungarvon Stream
They would whoop and make a noise whenever she would scream.
Boisetown, Ludlow, Astle, and always MacAdame
She set the hearts a-singing in the Valley Miramichi.

And there's never been another who could a sing her mournful tune
Her night light was brighter than a Dungarvon moon.
I can still see her shining in the Miramichi sun
In our land of many legends Old Dungarvon's number one.
"What do they call her?" said a stranger passing by

"She's the Dungarvon Whooper" was the sage reply.
Is she any louder when a crowd is gathered round?
She loves to watch their faces when she makes that mournful sound.
She would show up at the station and fill their hearts with glee
We were proud to call her "ours" through the Valley Miramichi.

In nineteen hundred thirty-six she made her final run
The days of steam were over, days of diesel had begun.
She brought joy to every heart and a smile to every face
And none before or after could ever take her place.
And there's never been another who could sing her mournful tune
Her night light was much brighter than a Dungarvon moon.
I can still see her shining in the Miramichi sun
In our land of many legends Old Dungarvon's number one.

It Takes All Sorts

Serendipity on the Banks of the Kennebecasis

Serendipity is the best assistant a researcher can have. Over the many years that I have been writing, serendipity has certainly led to some great stories. One of those moments happened when I was in the Legislative Library in Fredericton one winter day and I found under "Pamphlets—Music" a piece of sheet music from 1932 titled "On the Banks of the Kennebecasis," by Alfred George Clark. The cover had three photos of the Kennebecasis taken by H. W. B. Smith of Sussex, along with information that the piece had been published for the composer by Whaley, Royce & Company of 237 Young Street, Toronto, and sold at a price of forty cents, or three copies for one dollar. It was available from the author, whose address was given as Apohaqui PO, Kings County, NB.

My first thought was that the group I sing with, the Carleton Choristers, might be interested in performing this piece. They weren't.

My second thought was that perhaps, just perhaps, Mr. Clark might still be alive. He wasn't.

Nonetheless, I did get the song sung, and I got to meet

David Goss as A. G. Clark.

Mr. Clark and take on his persona for a short time when the song was performed by an ad hoc choral group. All because one serendipitous moment led to another.

It all started to happen in July of 2003, when Horace Macaulay's book *Historical Writings of Lower Millstream* came to my attention. Much to my delight, in the first few pages of personal recollections Macaulay mentioned taking music lessons from Alfred. George Clark. Further, he noted that the one piece of music he recalled was "On the Banks of the Kennebecasis." Serendipity? You bet.

In his recollections Macauley wrote,

All of us were given music lessons.... I can remember Murray [his brother] bringing the horse and rake from the hayfield when the music professor arrived. The horse would stand in the shade of the lawn until Murray's lesson was over. The tutor was Alfred G. Clark from Apohaqui. We used to comment on his inability to hear what we were saying, but he certainly did not miss each incorrect note as you struggled through your lesson. He also tuned pianos in the area and composed words and music which were printed as song sheets.

Of course, there was much more interest in the book, but when I reviewed it for the *New Brunswick Reader*, I included a footnote asking if anyone could shed more light on the man I was interested in, Alfred G. Clark. Serendipity hit again! A neighbour of Clark, Russ Bartlett, saw the story and called to say he had "mountains of memories of Daddy Clark," adding, "That's what we used to call him." He also said, "I think I can collect some memories from my family and share them with you." And he did just that on three occasions in the following year.

At our first meeting in late winter of 2004, he began by saying, "I appreciate you getting my mind back to these times. These memories are among the best part of my past. There are ten in the family. He was seventy when I was born. You don't get to know anybody till you are six or seven and I was twelve or thirteen when he died in 1963. So I only knew him for a short time, but those were the best times. He was like a grandfather."

It was a sentiment I was to hear several more times from Russ's siblings.

Russ told me that he did not remember Clark's wife, as she had died and Clark was living alone in a cottage next door to the Bartletts' home, just about opposite the Church of the Ascension at Apohaqui, on what was then the main road to Saint John from Sussex.

As he recalled it, there weren't people coming and going for music lessons at that time, and none of his brothers and sisters took lessons. "I never heard him play or sing, but there was lots of evidence of his musical background. There was an accordion—one with the wooden plugs. There used to be an old flute, and a horn. He never talked about it, but he probably had two thousand copies of that "On the Banks of the Kennebecasis" around the house. They were stacked in piles around his books. He had rooms and rooms of books, everything on shelves. He wrote mysteries. He had stacks of manuscripts. I don't think he had anything published. He had that song published, so he certainly might have. I know that he had just about every ten-cent mystery, and every magazine. Never threw nothing away," Russ recalled with a laugh.

Clark's pack-rat ways were attractive to Russ, and are likely the reason he has such a passion for collecting and antiques to this day. He explained, "To me, he lived in a gigantic house—lots of rooms. He only lived in a couple. There were rooms with nothing but books; rooms with nothing but bottles. Just a treasure trove of mystery for kids. I used to spend hours there, in the old magazines, just reading. Just thumbing through them, just fascinated with it. Every one of them were in order, tied up in little bundles, and put away. He was great at telling stories."

One story Russ recalled might have happened in England when Mr. Clark was a young man, Russ believes. "He told me he was on something like a footbridge, and it was very black and foggy, and dark. He got on this bridge, and he felt the presence of something.

He kept going and he was feeling around, and he got his hands on a set of horns. When you are a kid and he's telling you this, you're just terrified. Well, it was a bull. He said that he thought it was the devil coming for him."

Sharing this story reminded Russ of an incident where he turned the tables and scared Mr. Clark badly. "This one time, I was about nine and went to his house, and he was there and he had a table and it was just rounded with papers. He practically went from the bed to the rocking chair and to the table and put these big puzzles together. He was doing one of these puzzles, and I came in real quiet and yelled in his ear as loud as I could, 'MR. CLARK.' He turned around; I could never forget the look on his face. He chuckled. This is how we communicated. I wrote it out. 'Did you hear me?' He replied, 'I certainly did, I thought it was the good Lord himself calling me.'"

As far as Russ knows, Clark had no family in Canada, but he's sure there were relatives in England. "He wrote letters all the time to England, and he got mail from England. I think he must have been from England."

Clark apparently had a passion for games of all kinds. "He used to do these great big puzzles, crossword puzzles," Russ explained. "He'd open them up, bigger than a newspaper. He'd sit there by the hour, and talk about the winnings." And like many Canadians in the days before legal gambling, Clark played the Irish sweepstakes, according to Russ. He's not aware if Clark ever won, or what the man lived on, but he can say that "money did not seem to be a problem, though Mr. Clark was careful."

He added, "He depended on us to run errands and we used to get a nickel for our chores. He always paid a nickel. That would buy you a bag of chips. If you went to Jones Brothers in Apohaqui, a very big store, you'd get a dime, and a note for what he wanted. His writing was something else. He used to always put on his note, '10¢ for the bearer.' I never knew what that meant. You'd take that note over, and they'd ask, 'Are you the bear?' and laugh at us before you got your dime."

When Clark needed groceries, kerosene, wood laths for his fire, or a pail of water, he had a signal for Russ and his family. "He'd hang a orange package of some type in his window that Mom could see. In the family, we seem to be having difficulty remembering what it was. My sisters say that it was packaging from light bulbs that used to come in orange packaging, but I think it was King Cole Tea packages. Anyway, he'd hang three of these orange packages in the window, and Mom would say, 'Go see what Mr. Clark wants.'"

Russ's sisters would respond to calls for assistance, too, and they also have warm memories of Clark. His sister Ruth recalled, "Mom used to send us over with a plate of food. The house was always dark. He never threw a cig butt away. He would roll up three or four butts to make a cig. One day I tried one and I got as high and dizzy as a kite. Never did that again! I think he knew it would fix me for ever asking for another one. He never shaved. I think he must have cut his beard to keep it short. I used to cut his hair. If I hadn't seen him for a few days, he'd always say, 'pussy cat, pussy cat, where have you been?' He was the grandfather we never had, and us older kids thought the world of him."

"One time," she added, "We took him over home to look at the TV. He just looked and said, 'I'll just keep reading my paper.'"

Russ and Ruth's other sister Georgie also has great memories of the old man, including a scare she once got as a result of Clark hobbling on a crutch in his later years. Of his crutches, she said, "Prof. Clark was struck by a car after dark. That is why he used crutches. I remember when I was just a little girl walking to school and he was standing outside his door and he had on a long black sweater and had long grey hair. He never spoke, just stood there like a ghost. It scared me so much, I began to run."

Gail, another of the Bartlett clan, added to the reminiscences: "I have always had very fond memories of my childhood, living in Apohaqui as a middle child in a family of five boys and five girls, but one of my fondest memories was all the time I spent with Professor Clark. He really made us kids feel special. He was very much the most eccentric grandfather anyone could have. We didn't think a thing of the way he dressed which was very extraordinary to say the least. I think that if he got a hole in his clothes he just layered on more. His vest hung way below his waist. His pants hung like feed sacks."

She continued, "He heated his house with an old coal stove in the back room. He lived in the front of the house in basically two small rooms. It was very dark. The curtains hung on the windows like shreds of smoky grey lace. His bed was piled high with quilts. Brass candlesticks stood like sentinels on the old fireplace mantle. We never questioned why he did not have hydro. It just seemed normal to us that he didn't. He never went out to visit anyone and as far as we knew, no one except us kids next door visited him. He would cut up newspapers in little strips, and when he wanted to light one of his homemade cigarettes or cigars—I'm not sure what they were—he would fold his strips and put it down inside the chimney of the old oil lamp. I'm sure my younger brother who was about eight at the time knew what they were, because I think he smoked his first with old Professor Clark. He was always Professor Clark to us. I think I thought it was his actual first name. He was just the nicest friend we ever had."

Besides their memories of feeling special in Clark's presence, the Bartlett children also recall with fondness the treats he offered. Russ said, "Anything sweet was a treat for us in those days and Mr. Clark had lots of sweets. He always had jelly beans in his pocket. They were soft. We loved them. Never ever turned down a jellybean. Another thing that he used to do was offer us Velveeta cheese. He had an old knife, and he'd leave a chunk of cheese on that knife right across the box. We never asked for it, but any time we saw it, we were to have it."

Oxo cubes were another treat, Russ recalled, "He used to have a mug that had a dog on it, it came from Quaker Oats. He put an Oxo cube in it and some milk, and I think he put some sort of cream in it. He never washed that cup. It was a quarter-inch thick [with scum] on the sides. We'd go in there and we'd drink that down. It was some good."

Clark also gave the children little newspaper hats that he folded. Russ recalled, "You'd open the hat and there would be a treat in it."

In October of 2004, based on the interviews with the Bartlett family, I was able to impersonate Alfred George Clark for the singers at the annual Fall Workshop of the New Brunswick Choral Federation at Kings Landing. As Russ played his guitar and sang some songs he'd written about the Apohaqui area, I came hobbling into the little Presbyterian Church dressed as Clark and told his story as Russ and his siblings had shared it with me. Then I told about the song he had written, "On the Banks of the Kennebecasis," complained that it was rarely performed anymore, and asked if the group of singers would try a real New Brunswick song from the way-back times.

Sara Kennedy, the executive director of the choral federation was in on the scenario, and had the music all ready, and so the choristers agreed to sing the song. At that point, the serendipity seemed to end, as they didn't like the song much. I had to agree that it is a hard piece to sing. Nevertheless, I was content to hear it sung a couple of times, and I was happy that everyone had enjoyed meeting Russ and hearing his stories of Alfred George Clark as much as I had. Serendipity had led us to that point, and serendipity may yet add further twists to this story. But for now, here are the words that Alfred George Clark wrote:

1.

On the banks of the Kennebecasis, where the many waters meet;
I am sitting with my dearest one, Where the trout play at my feet,
There's a salmon pool below me, Where the wild duck dip and dive.
'Tis a paradise for sportsmen, and 'tis bliss to be alive.

Chorus
Apohaqui, where the millstream and the Kennebecasis meet;
Sing with the waters, play and daydream, at a place you cannot beat.
Pack up a lunch box, come to Moncton, Take the 2 Route to Saint John,
Tickle a trout brook, And at night say, "O boys!, that was one sweet day."

2.

On the twining shining highway, brilliant cars flash back the sun,
Down from Moncton as they roll along. To Saint John a tip-top run,
Thro' the valley fair, Valhalla, ever fairer as they go.
Ev'ry town will give them welcome, with a smile to see them come.

3.

In the forest, true primeval, there is lure and charm for all
And the pine woods of fair CANADA sound a thrilling hunters' call
Virgin forests, sloping mountains, smiling lakes and waterfalls
All the beauties of the by lanes, sing a song which never palls.

4.

And at night when shades are falling, from the bridges we can see
Where the moonlit silver pathway, shimmers clear down to the sea
For never do we part as we roll along our way
On the banks a winding, winding, silver wavelets thrill our heart.

5.

I am singing of the beauties, of the road to old SAINT JOHN
In the Kennebecasis valley, everyone will know the song
Leave depression, and contention, for a while to take their course
Breathe the ozone, take vacation, in the wild woods of the north.

Lectures and Lobsters and Bethell and Books

There aren't too many places in New Brunswick where you can go to find a large selection of books and be assured of a free three-, ten-, or twenty-minute lecture every time you drop into the shop. For that, you have to skip the big chain bookstores and go straight to a lobster-covered bungalow in downtown Miramichi city. There, you'll find the Lobster Man himself, John Bethell, with his collection of authentic lobster creations and some twenty thousand books. If you're lucky, you'll see him wearing one of the many lobster T-shirts or other apparel items he has for sale, like the lobster claw hat or the full-body lobster suit, and you'll get his full lecture. It's a busy business that he's built up around the shells of the favourite seafood of many Canadians—the lobster, or, as he'll tell you, the creature "properly known as homarus americanus."

It's sure not what he started out to do, but he's dedicated to it nevertheless. "I don't believe in retirement. I'll be running this store and making lobster creations till I'm a hundred if I hit that," he told me with a laugh. He began life in North Sydney, graduated from UNB in 1964 with an engineering degree, and entered the military, where he became a captain in the air force at the Chatham base. He married a local girl; settled down; taught math, physics, and chemistry at Miramichi High for a dozen years; wrote a weekly newspaper column; and self-trained as a taxidermist. "One day at Baie St-Anne I saw lobster shells made into a fisherman. It wasn't that good a job, and I thought I could do better, so I tried it," he explained. Since then, he's made thousands. "Any character you can name, I can make," he said.

Looking over the shop's stock, you can see that this is no idle boast, for, besides the ubiquitous fishermen, there are hunters of every type, Santas in various forms, brides and grooms, Elvis reincarnations, and his favourite (at the moment) and most appropriate to the Miramichi, the leprechaun.

John Bethell reveals his Lobster Man identity.

Getting to this point has been a gradual process. In 1977, with his interest in teaching waning, he came to the realization that the "ultimate is working for yourself," and decided to open a souvenir store. In 1990 he decided to build on his love for books by adding these to his business. As he explained, "I had started a personal collection, and running the bookstore there isn't a day that goes by that I don't find some treasure from the books that come through the door." So many come through, in fact, that he's about to expand the shop so that he can have more books on display in the store and get rid of some of the seven outbuildings in which he now stores his stock.

In addition to all those books, visitors to his store also get one of John's famous lectures. He can—and does—talk on a wide range of topics, as he speed reads most everything that passes through the shop: "I can glean the most important points with a quick look," he told me. Most of his lectures, though, are about lobster. Using a wall map of the Maritimes, he shows where lobsters live, explains how they talk, how and when they mate, where and when they are caught, how they are processed. "That is where I gets the shells I use for my creations," he explained as he shows boxes full of shells ready to be wired and hot glued into statues ranging from miners to ministers, bingo to ball players.

Using a huge male lobster as a visual aid, he gave me a rapid-fire explanation, never sure when he would have to stop to serve a customer. "What you call the tail is the abdomen.... This is the ripper claw, this is the crusher.... Look at this row of teeth, here's the mouth, do you want to see the Virgin Mary?... How about how to tell the male from the female?... Do you know how to hypnotize a lobster?..." And so on.

"I like to tell people how to kill them humanely, and how to get the best and most meat," he told me. "You know, people have an awful lot of misconceptions about the lobster, and I try to clear up a bit of it, even if I only have a few minutes."

If you're ever on the Miramichi, a visit to John Bethell's store is time well spent. You're sure to learn something new about New Brunswick's history and way of life from this one-of-a-kind shopkeeper and craftsman.

Bowling for Records

When a Saint John event gets a front-page column in a New York newspaper, that's news. And two Saint John men made that news happen in 1933 when they took part in a two-hundred-string marathon bowling event at the Central Alleys on King Street. The dates were February 8 and 9 and the men were Walter R. Golding, manager of the Saint John Trojans and one of Saint John's best-known sports, and Donald S. McCavour, one of the best bowlers in the city at the time. McCavour was the only sportsman in the city who was willing to take part in the marathon event dreamed up by Golding.

Donald S. McCavour (left) and Walter R. Golding (right) each bowled for more than twenty hours at Central Alley on King Street, Saint John.

The newspaper that reported their feat was the now-defunct *New York World Telegram*, which carried the story on the front page, in column six, under the title "Bowled Over." The story, bearing the subhead "Bowler collapses after knocking down 20,595 consecutive pins," read as follows:

Credit Donald S. McCavour and Walter R. Golding with something new in the way of endurance tests. They started bowling candlepins at midnight Wednesday, setting up as their objective 200 consecutive strings within a time limit of 25 hours. McCavour finished with 20,595 pins in 20 hours and forty minutes; Golding with 20,044 in 21 hours. Each hurled almost 6000 balls. McCavour collapsed at the finish and had to be taken home in a taxi. Golding walked home.

While it was nice to see a New Brunswick story in the New York paper, it took some digging through local papers of the era to bring the whole story into clearer focus.

Walter R. Golding was by profession one of the first distributors of motion pictures in the Maritimes and the proprietor of the Community Theatre in West Saint John. By avocation he was one of the most ardent sportsmen and sports promoters of the 1920s. He also founded the Trojan athletic empire, which included champion teams in a number of sports. His particular favourite was the Trojan Basketball Club, which was the team to beat in Eastern Canadian basketball circles from its formation in 1921 till 1936. Golding also managed football, baseball, and hockey clubs, and occasionally promoted boxing cards. He regularly loaned his business acumen to groups in the community who were organizing minor sports activities.

Throughout his life, Golding was an ardent bowler, and he especially enjoyed marathon bowling events. In 1932 he had completed a one-hundred-string marathon, averaging ninety-seven pins per string, which was considered a Maritime record. Sometime after that challenge, he issued an invitation to Saint John bowlers to try for a world record of two-hundred strings in twenty-four hours. Donald

S. McCavour was the only bowler brave enough to answer Golding's challenge.

McCavour was a well-known sports figure too. He had played basketball, football, and baseball throughout the Maritimes, and was both a pupil and competitor of the famed oarsman Hilton Belyea. McCavour was a regular bowler at the Central Alleys, and in league competition he was averaging 101 at the time of the marathon. Reports said he bowled a fast ball after taking a short run, which was directly opposite to Golding's style of rolling a slow ball from an upright position.

The match began at midnight on Wednesday, February 8, 1933, at the Central Alleys, with pin boys working six-hour shifts to keep the one-and-three-quarter-inch candlepins in position. There was a large crowd of spectators even at that late hour, and they continued to come throughout the following twenty-four hours to cheer on the bowlers. Among the crowd were many scoffers who doubted either man would finish the two hundred strings they had set as their goal. Before noon on Thursday, both men had reached one hundred strings, with McCavour leading Golding by 407 pins and their averages being 100 and 103, respectively. Both were reported to be haggard but determined to continue.

As they bowled, both men drank orange juice, water, and coffee, and munched on sandwiches. The only break was for necessary bathroom privileges, and when that occurred, a substitute stepped in to pace the remaining bowler. They weren't even allowed the five-minute breaks that are standard in marathon events these days! Under these conditions, McCavour finished his two hundred strings on Thursday evening at 8:40 PM, after knocking down 20,595 pins and averaging 102. He then sat down to watch Walter Golding finish his last few strings. Suddenly, McCavour fell over, unable to stay awake any longer. Spectators carried him out of the alley and sent him home in a taxi. Golding continued to bowl, and by nine o'clock had completed his goal of two-hundred, knocking down either 20,044 pins (according to the *New York World Telegram*) or 20,049 (according

A NEW PLAY

4 O'clock

By

NAN O'REILLY and RUPERT DARRELL

Management of

CHARLES HENDERSON

LONGACRE THEATRE
220 West 48th Street

CHickering
4-4200-1

New
New York N.Y.

Feb 11th/33

Dear Mr Golden

It is the consensus of opinion in New Hork. That owing to the fact you were able to walk home after the contest, It makes you the winner

Congratulations on putting St John on the front page

Very truly

Chas Henderson

The letter from Charles Henderson naming Walter Golding as the champion.

to the *Saint John Times Globe*), for an average of just over 100. He then walked to his nearby uptown lodgings for a well-earned rest.

Who won the match? By pin total it was McCavour; by sheer endurance, Golding. It was Golding who received a congratulatory letter a few days later from Charles Henderson, manager of the Longacre Theatre, 200 West 48th Street, New York, which read, "Dear Mr. Golden [yes, he spelled it wrong], It is the consensus of opinion in New York that owing to the fact you were able to walk home after the contest, it makes you the winner. Congratulations on putting St. John on the front page. Very Truly, Chas Henderson."

Many bowlers of the time thought that Golding and McCavour were crazy to try such a stunt, but these doubters had to doff their hats when the two actually succeeded. Likewise, many people doubted that anyone would ever break the record the two had set, but records seem to stand for just that purpose. Today's Canadian record holder is an Australian, Suresh Joachim, who bowled for one hundred hours straight, from June 8 to 12, 2005, in Toronto.

Nonetheless, Golding and McCavour were the champions of their day, and they had the blistered fingers, stiff muscles, and wearied bodies to prove it. As the years passed, if anyone doubted their championship status, they not only had local bowlers who could attest to their feats, but also that clipping in the *New York World Telegram*, which told the world of the new record two determined Saint Johners had set.

Old Holt the Miser Kept Them Guessing... Alive and Dead

One thing that can be said with certainty about Isaac Oulton (1813–1902), known by all as Old Holt the Miser, is that he kept the people of North End Saint John guessing throughout the time he lived among them, for all but seven years from the late 1830s till his curious death in April 1902. Even after his death, he seemed to taunt the locals with his appearance as a ghost near the hovel in which he lived on the corner of Douglas Avenue and Main Street. And when portions of a treasure map showed up among the piles of debris in that ramshackle house, they fed the longstanding suspicion that he was not destitute, but only played the part in order to protect the gold he had procured when he made a trip to the gold fields of California during the rush of 1849.

Old Holt's house was located in the space of this now vacant lot at the corner of Douglas Avenue and Main Street, Saint John.

Upon his return from the west in 1857, he spoke of having accumulated twenty thousand dollars, which he claimed to have placed among the banks for safekeeping. Banks did not seem to be the sort of place Oulton would place his money, so a general belief grew that he had hidden it about his home, or in some other secure but remote location. On his return from California, he was described as a "good looking man of about 40 years of age...of prosperous appearance... with good clothes notably a stylish Panama hat." The hat was the only bit of the "prosperity" look he retained till the end of his days.

From papers found in his home after his death, it was clear he invested some of his money in land speculation in the Lancaster area and also near his home in the North End. The investments went sour, though there is no indication in the available information of just why this happened. Thereafter he took up the pedalling trade, though he rarely showed signs of having any money in his pockets. He would be seen with great regularity scavenging at the Elm Street dump, near his home, for both goods and foods, and in his later years he would augment what he could get in the dump by begging meals wherever he was made welcome. And many made him welcome, hoping he might reveal the location of his treasury.

Despite his apparent impoverished condition, about ten years after returning from the gold fields, he managed to secure a wife and for a time lived in the Mahogany Road area on the west side of the city. A report in the *Coin Collector's Journal* of January 1884 described a visit made to the Oulton household, out the Mahogany Road, by a solicitor identified only as "Mr. H." Mr. H. described how he took a friend to the Oulton house, telling him he would be visiting "an old miser, half lunatic," who he assured him was worth fifty thousand dollars yet lived frugally. Upon their arrival, it took several knocks before they heard the sound of someone who "withdrew bolts and bars" and "slowly opened the door." But Oulton did not welcome his callers, and in fact firmly told them, "I don't want no callers, what be ye after?"

When the solicitor explained he had a friend who was looking to buy some old coins, they were let in, and introduced to Oulton's wife, a Mrs. Bishop, whom he described as a "tall gaunt women" who had just prepared their supper. It was described as a simple meal consisting of "a bowl of melted fat and a great platter of Indian mush." As his wife held a flickering candle, Oulton led the visitors to a dark anteroom stacked with "expensive furniture, but none of it used." Oulton then pulled out a treasure chest hidden in the pile of furnishings, and after rifling through "curiosities of all kinds, for Old Holt had been a great traveller in his day," came to several coins the pair were able to buy.

When Oulton's wife died, he did not bother with funeral arrangements. In keeping with his character, he placed her body in a wheelbarrow, pushed it two kilometres to the Carleton Cemetery, and took care of the burial himself.

In 1882 he ran for public office as a councillor on a platform of strict economy. He did not get elected, though his nomination papers were signed by some "distinguished names." Sometime after that, he moved to 41 Douglas Avenue and began filling the house with goods he scavenged on daily trips to nearby dumps. He somehow found and brought a new bride to the house, and they lived very privately, even turning away those claiming to be relatives, always, it seems, suspicious that someone would find his money and steal it.

As he shuffled about the city, Old Holt was tormented by kids and harassed by adults who hoped he would reveal the location of the gold everyone thought he had. Rocks would be thrown through his windows at night, and threatening notes were delivered to his home from time to time. After his second wife died, he became more reclusive. He was then almost ninety. When he was found dead in his home by the Gillespie family, the police could not decide if the death was accidental or just made to look that way. The case was never solved.

Oulton's mysterious death soon gave rise to further speculation, as reported in the *Daily Sun* of May 7, 1902:

That a house with such a sinister history as the scene of the Oulton trag-edy should acquire the reputation of being haunted is natural, but nobody expected it so soon. Perhaps it is because the appearance of the place is so in keeping with all ghostly tradition; for certainly there never was a house more peculiarly fitted inside and out for the accommodation of a shade of the morbid variety, than this.

At any rate tremulous wispers already tell of eerie nightime happen-ings in and about that squalid, filth encumbered hovel, whose walls have hidden so much of mystery and blood. Already belated pedestrians tiptoe fearfully past its grim front as they hurry home, and even in broad day-light the passer-by looks askance at its boarded up windows and barred doors and loaf no more than is necessary in that vicinity. And already those may be found who will hint darkly about mysterious flickering lights seen late at night through the chinks of the kitchen window and who will whisper with half-held breath of muffled moans distinctly heard on more than one occasion by someone who told somebody else, whose friend told a friend of the informant.

The policemen who guarded the house night and day claimed they had not noticed anything weird or out of the ordinary, but that did not reassure the people of Saint John, who continued to be sus-picious of the property for years to come. And they continued to believe the old miser's fortune would show up there, or in some other location. Their belief was piqued by a report in the *Star* of April 25, 1902, which read:

Among the papers found in the house of Isaac G. Oulton was one yellow with age and bearing many thumb marks that is of more than ordinary interest. It is a plain and simple diagram which apparently locates a trea-sure chest near the city, and in many ways it smacks of the stories of Capt. Kidd's treasures and the chests guarded by dead men's bones. The local situation gives an added interest to this plan that is wanting elsewhere.

According to the *Star*, the map seemed to point to the banks of Little River, an area that had long been suspected of harbouring buried treasure. "It may be that Mr. Oulton's plans may help some eager seeker to obtain his heart's desire," predicted the *Star*.

No one ever did find the miser's buried treasure. Thus, in death, as in life, Isaac Oulton was a man of mystery.

Campobello's Last Hermit

When many people hear the words "Campobello" and "hermit" together, they think of the nom de plume taken by Admiral William Fitz-William Owen. After a long and successful career as a naval officer and hydrographer that began at age fourteen, he concluded, when fifty-nine, that his "worldly ambition was barred by corruption in high places," and retired to the family estate his father had

Murray Alexander with his sketch of Will Calder, a Campobello hermit.

founded on Campobello. Seven years later, in 1841, a Boston publisher issued a book generally considered to be Owen's thinly disguised memoirs, *The Quoddy Hermit, or Conversations at Fairfield on Religion and Superstition*. And thus began the fame of the Hermit of Campobello.

However, he was not the only Campobello hermit, as I have learned in conversation with several island residents on visits over the past couple of summers. The other was Will Calder, known as the "Hermit of Meadow Brook." Dan Anthony first told me the story and took me to visit May Newman, who did not know Will, but knew of him through her husband, Wilfred Newman.

"I met my husband in Scotland and came here as a war bride to Welshpool in 1945," May told me. "Wilfred had tried to tell me what Campobello was like, but it was a shock to arrive on the mailboat and see the few houses that made up Welshpool. I had come from a town outside Glasgow named Johnstone, about fifty thousand people and lots of industry."

Will Calder died in 1943, before May's husband returned from war service. He is buried in an unmarked grave at the Anglican Cemetery of St. Anne's Church. One of the tales Wilfred had shared with May was of his days as a youth at Meadow Brook, where he often went to spend time with Will Calder, the Hermit of Meadow Brook.

"Wilfred had great memories of Will, and told me how he fished there, and made oars, and sometimes walked into Welshpool to get his groceries, which he carried in a satchel back to Meadow Brook. He also carried oil for his lamps all that way. He walked everywhere and had paths he followed through the woods as there were no roads out that way in those days," she noted.

She shared two photos with me, one of Will Calder, pipe in mouth standing on a ramp in front of the shed in which he lived at Meadow Brook, and the other of Will Calder, Fred Cline, Buddy Cline, and her husband as a teen or young man, again in the doorway of the hermit's shed.

"I have been told that the old stove he cooked on was still there until a few years ago, in the bushes by the beach," she noted, and Danny agreed that this was so.

Later, May's brother-in-law, Lee Newman, added to the details. "I went out there from time to time, fishing for trout in the Meadow Brook. Will did not like trout at all, he preferred eels and he walked over to Eastern Pond, which is now dried up, and caught eels there. He would cook and eat them and we would cook our trout and eat them at the shed. He had a few lobster traps he set out, and he also made punts, and possibly sold them."

Both of them suggested Murray Alexander might have some recollections, and he did. As well, he had done sketches of Will and a painting of the view from the front window of Will's cabin. Murray had also written and recorded a recollection of the Meadow Brook Hermit, which he willingly shared. It read:

After years of going to sea in the big two master schooners, Will Calder, at age 30, went to his beloved Meadow Brook and lived to well over 80. A very hale and hearty 80 odd years, building boats (both full scale and models) and giving generously of his winsome spirit through tales of nature and folklore. Survival was a game to be played with eagerness and joyful anticipation. Tedium did not exist. He read papers (when he had them), hunted, fished. The brook held trout, the sea more plentiful fish than it does today. The fragrance of wood shaving in his large outer room and the fragrant pipe smoke were there, with the slow twinkling smile when several gold teeth glowed under the bristling moustache.

Of his tribute, Murray said, "I wrote this as every time I was out to Meadow Brook, wandering through the woodland and along the shore, I thought of my old friend and realized time was passing on, and I wanted to make sure I had his essence before I got older."

Murray said that he met Will in the cove in the forties when he and his brother would go out there. Will made them both model boats, but Murray no longer has his and does not know what happened to his brother's.

Murray and his brother were fascinated by the isolation and detachment they saw in Will. "When you walked out there," Murray recalled, "you looked down a valley as you neared Will's cabin, and you saw it surrounded by willows. Will would be sitting outside the cabin smoking his pipe, looking out to sea."

Murray continued, "As for the trail into the camp itself, it was so complicated you could easily get lost, and the inner trail seemed more like three miles than two. At Eastern Pond, where the tide comes in at one end of the bar—it could cut you off if you were unlucky enough to time it wrong—Will had a knotted rope that, tied to a tree twenty-five or thirty feet up the cliff, he used to use when the gap was full of water [to reach the big gravel bar]. It is a measure of how fit he was, that he still did this when quite old, for the rope came only about seven feet from the ground. Apparently he timed this according to the monthly highest tides. Once, when [Will] was near eighty, my brother visited him in early winter. Astounded upon return, he said Will had told him, 'I went back home late one cold night, down near zero, had to climb down the rope with a knapsack and slipped on the rope, or the rope gave way.' Will told him he fell into the rushing water, and while not too deep, he was soaked to his head, and had to trudge that last mile in bitter cold. 'Oh, well, I lit a good fire and finally got warmed up, took a while,' he said. Anyone else might have died of exposure, not Will!"

The camp itself had two double doors and windows on one side. It had a one-burner stove. It was surprisingly comfortable, with a kitchen-type straight-back chair in the main living area. There was an attached workroom, where he would build dinghies for the fishermen and the models boats he did as a hobby.

He cooked scones a lot and, if desperate, might even make a crow soup, Murray said. Will knew all the old cures, the natural ones the First Nations knew, Murray added, noting he would cook up barnacles as one of the cures, for stomach aches.

When Will got older, he got weak and had to be carried out from Meadow Brook on a stretcher. A kind couple took him in and he spent his last days with them at Wilson's Beach.

After reading a story I wrote about the Hermit of Meadow Brook, Paul Cline contacted me with even more fascinating information about this unique character. Will was very ingenious, he noted, speaking of a winch he made for his boat. "He had made a big log into a winch and had drilled holes in it, in which he could place a dowel-like piece of wood to hold the winch in position. This was used to wind in his dory."

For his water, Paul noted, "He had a well in the woods behind the camp at Meadow Brook and it was a bubbling spring, kept clean by a sixteen-inch trout that often lurked under a rock in the well."

At one time, Will kept a pet seal, Paul said, having gotten the seal as a pup and having befriended it. "It would drag itself up the beach to his camp and actually go right into the camp. It eventually wore off its skin on the hot rocks," he said.

"In summer, Will had a garden at the eastern side of Meadow Brook and there he raised potatoes and other vegetables," Paul noted. "For fishing, Will always had a fourteen-foot dory for hand lining. He once caught a ninety-two-pound halibut, and that was its dressed weight—no head, no tail, no guts. It was caught on a hand line."

Paul elaborated on Will's boatbuilding activities, saying, "He built punts, or square-ended boats. And the design was unusual, as they had high sternboards, so they could be landed in rough seas at Meadow Brook or elsewhere, I suppose. He also made oars and tholing pins [the pins that hold oars in place on a rowboat] and knit bait bags for lobster traps. He is known to have made at least two models of full-rigged, old-time sailing ships from memory of seeing them as a youngster."

Will was also a skilled hunter. Paul was once with him on a hunting expedition when they came to a huge birch tree in which there were five partridge roosting. Will shot them one by one with his .22, beginning with the one closest to the bottom. Asked why, he said, "Well, if I shot the one at the top first, and he tumbled down, the others would see him fall and fly away."

Paul also remembers Will's distinct smoking habits: "He had a pipe on the go constantly and if he was out of tobacco, he used a local plant to mix in with his store-bought tobacco, which he would cut and grind in with a knife, and then add in the plant, which he called 'tomawy.'"

Will had no use for modern apparatuses. Paul recalled that NB Tel had a relay station at the eastern side of Eastern Passage—something to do with getting the signal by cable over to Grand Manan. "This was a very remote location, subject to vandalism, or just storm damage, and they asked Will if he would keep his eye on it and report any problems to them. In return, they would run a phone line to his cabin. He turned down the phone line, saying he didn't want anything in the camp that would make a noise."

Will Calder, the Hermit of Meadow Brook, has been gone now for over half a century, but he has not been forgotten, nor is he liable to be, as long as there are Campobellians to tell his tale.

Paul Cline shares stories about Will Calder while sitting on a rock at Meadow Brook.

We Worked Hard—
We Played Hard

Making Ice the Old-Fashioned Way

Unlike most of us, John Dolan loved the hard, cold nights of January and February. He depended on such nights for his living; it was in those months that ice formed in the lakes around Saint John, ice that Dolan cut and sold through his firm, the Crystal Ice Company. Back in 1980, when he was eighty-four and had been retired for fifteen years, Dolan fondly recalled those days in the ice business for this author.

"There were busy years, and we worked hard," he said in an interview. And he gave the impression that he'd still be out on the lakes if there was a local demand for ice, but there wasn't, and hasn't been since mechanical refrigerators became affordable in the 1950s and the familiar ice truck disappeared from Saint John's streets. But

Before the widespread availability of mechanical refrigeration, ice was harvested from lakes. This man is using a pickaroon to manoeuvre a block of ice.

for thirty years before that, anyone who bought a block of ice in Saint John was likely getting the product from one of John Dolan's two ice houses at Mystery Lake and Dolan Lake. The two lakes in the Golden Grove area of Saint John East provided most of the ice for Dolan's customers. Besides the residential customers served by his delivery trucks, there were accounts like the Saint John Market, the hospitals, and the meat and fish stores served by five other trucks.

Mr. Dolan got into the ice business in 1925 because he didn't want to farm like his father had. Yet, in speaking of his years in the business, he often referred to "harvesting the ice" or "harvesting the crop"—terms a farmer would use. Actually, ice production, when carried out under the watchful eye of Board of Health officials, is not far removed from farming. As Mr. Dolan described the operation, "In the fall of the year we'd drain Mystery Lake dry. There'd only be a brook running through it. William Pugsley had built a dam on the lake with the intention of constructing a power plant, but that never worked out. But the dam made it possible for us to drain the lake every year. Then we'd clean the bottom, cut all the weeds and brush, and then close the dam and let the lake fill up again. In later years, the Board of Health requirements were such that we had to construct a chlorine station where the water ran into the lake, and add chlorine so the water, when frozen, would test perfectly safe for human consumption."

His method of harvesting the ice was not unique for the times, though not a soul today would know how to go about it. "Firstly," he explained, "we had to wait until the ice was fourteen to fifteen inches thick, and that was generally right after the New Year. If there was snow on the lake we'd scrape it off to the side, and then we'd set the mechanical saw in operation. It consisted of a motor which was mounted on skids, which drove a large saw blade set about four feet in front of the motor.

"It was controlled by two men who pushed it along the ice, making cuts into the ice, so we ended up with chunks of ice twenty-two inches by thirty-two inches by about fourteen to eighteen inches deep. These pieces were floated to a mechanical lifter, known as the runway. Sometimes a man would stand on the cut ice and float it to the runway; other times the men would guide it into place by standing on the shore and use pickaroons to move it to the runway.

"It really didn't matter so long as the large ice floes got to the runway. There, they were picked out of the water by a mechanical conveyor belt, and as the ice passed up the runway to the ice house, it was shaved so that all pieces were of uniform thickness. The ice house itself stood a few yards from the shore of the lake, and was three stories in height, and the runway leading from the lake to the ice house was adjustable so that as the ice house filled up, the runway was raised."

He noted that the runway was removed from the water at night so it wouldn't freeze too hard. Explaining how the icehouse kept the ice frozen throughout the warm days of summer, he said: "One of our icehouses was two hundred feet long, and it was divided into six thirty-foot rooms. Each room was separated by a double boarded wall in which twelve inches of sawdust was placed as insulation. The outside walls were similarly constructed. The top of the ice would be covered by twelve inches of straw. There was only a little shrinkage at the top and along the sides using this method no matter how hot it got in summer."

Home consumers never received the twenty-two-by-thirty-two blocks, which weighed a whopping four hundred pounds. Instead, a cutter would chop the block into eight fifty-pound chunks, just right for the home icebox. It took about four weeks to cut and store all the ice he required for his customers. However, he noted that during World War II demand for ice was so great that it took two extra weeks to cut and an additional icehouse had to be built to store it. Some ice from Dolan and Mystery Lakes was known to have been shipped as far west as British Columbia in aid of the war effort. Huge quantities were used in Saint John in refrigerating meat destined for the troops overseas.

"Sometimes," Dolan said, "there would be as many as eight hundred railcars of meat awaiting shipment from Saint John, and the vessel destined to carry the meat overseas would never arrive. We'd have to stock the reefer cars with ice while they stood in the rail yards until another ship could be found to take the meat.

"In fact," he continued, "there was such a demand for our ice that the employees of the company were not considered for service overseas, and during the spring weight restrictions on the roadways, Crystal Ice trucks were allowed to travel fully loaded."

After the war, however, demand for ice began to drop off as a more affluent society began purchasing refrigerators, and commercial operations installed their own refrigeration or ice-making equipment. Eventually, the Saint John operation ceased, but Crystal Ice still manufactured ice in Moncton and Halifax for some years.

Even if energy costs skyrocketed and mechanical ways became too expensive, Dolan could not imagine a return to the old methods of harvesting ice when he told his story in 1980. "Today," he said, "it would be difficult to find workers who would endure the cold, the occasional spills into the lake, and the seasonal nature of the work. Times were different then. I started business when lots of workers were available, I worked a lake that was right for ice harvesting and I had a product people needed."

Clinton Guptill Spins a Seagoing Yarn

Clinton Guptill's home overlooks the wide expanse of the Saint John River at Dominion Park in Saint John West. It seems as appropriate a location as possible for a man who grew up on Grand Manan, went out fishing at fifteen, and then spent his life on fishing boats, ferries, and rescue tugboats in the Bay of Fundy and on the high seas around the world. He'd love to be back on Grand Manan, but life at sea has been curtailed by the onset of health problems that make it sensible to be as close to medical care as possible.

He was delighted when I introduced him to a poem called "The Sailor's Consolation," an old Victorian piece by Charles Dibdin that expresses many a seafarer's sentiments exactly. Dibdin wrote of a hurricane where "the sea was mountains rolling" and of "fool-hardy chaps who live in towns" and "what dangers they are hauling, and now are quaking in their beds for fear the roof should fall in." In contrast, he noted, the sailors at sea "on the deck are comfortably lying."

"That's exactly what my dad would tell us when we were fishing off Grand Manan and a blow came up," Clinton laughed. He still goes to Grand Manan as often as possible to visit with his fellow fishermen and sailors and to share "yyyaaarrrnnnsss." And Clinton has no end of seafaring yyyaaarrrnnnsss—as you will see as you read on.

Explaining how he got started as a seafarer, Clinton told me, "We were only fifteen and we decided we were going fishing, and mother said that we were staying in school and we told her we weren't—that's my twin brother and I—and she said, 'I'll get the Mountie to take you, and you'll stay there all day.' We said, 'When he leaves, we leave.' So dad took us fishing with him, and gave us enough bad weather and bad fishing so that we'd go back to school again. We spent all winter fishing flounder between Campobello and Eastport. Cold, my it was cold. He thought that would drive us back to school. He didn't want us to go fishing.

Don't call Grand Mananer Clinton Guptill a Nova Scotian!

He wanted us to get an education, and we wanted to go fishing. We stayed with him fishing till 1956."

After three years with his dad, Clinton moved to Saint John and found work with the Saint John Tugboat Company, which was owned at the time by Charlie Wilson. There he had his first rescue adventure.

"Wilson got a call saying that Pier 12 was on fire, and it was full of jute and carpets. There was a ship there, the *City of London*, which had just come in from India with a full load. We steamed down the harbour and the smoke was so thick that you couldn't tell there was a ship there. We went in and found the ship, hooked to the bow of her and backed off, parted her lines off the wharf. We got her down to Pier 13 or 14 and they dropped anchor. The lifeboat on the port side was burned off or melted, and even the portholes going into the accommodations were melted. Mr. Wilson put in a salvage claim against her. I don't know how much money he got, but about three years later Keith Wilson called and asked me to come over to the office. Mr. Wilson gave me a cheque for two hundred and fifty dollars. It was quite a present just before Christmas."

Following that, Clinton went with the Irving Companies, where he did ocean towing and had his fair share of adventures, including one occasion in 1957 when he was sent to tow a ship from Havana, Cuba, to Tampa, Florida. "They could only use a Canadian tug, as the Americans would not go, and the Russians were too far away, so we got the job of towing from Havana to Florida," he explained. "It was the sister ship to one that I had towed out of the Gulf a couple years earlier. It had more bedbugs on it than I had ever seen—and cockroaches, oh golly! We went aboard her just to see the cockroaches," he laughed.

During those years, he also worked out of Saint John on some of the river tugs, but eventually he left Irving and went back to Grand Manan to fish. He then worked on the Grand Manan ferry as a deckhand, a wenchman, a second mate, a first mate, and finally as the captain. He was also a mate and captain of the *Princess of Acadia*, which sailed between Saint John and Digby.

Of these experiences, Clinton said, "I figured that in time you could train a monkey to do that job. Put a stock of bananas on each port and he'd go back and forth to get them. It didn't have the challenge of going to sea and making a rescue. Of seeing how good you could be at it, see if you could be as good as anybody else, or better than anybody else."

So he returned to work on the tugs, and this decision led to his ultimate adventure on the *Terra Nova Sea*, a 150-foot vessel with ten thousand horsepower, in November 1994. That rescue netted him an Award of Merit for Lifesaving with Risk of Life, the highest medal available from Saint John Ambulance. The award was presented at a reception in Nova Scotia's Government House by Lieutenant-Governor James Kinley. His all-Canadian crew were also honoured and received gold rings from the tug's owner, Secunda Marine.

The story began at 1:00 AM on November 5, 1994, when Clinton received a call at his Saint John home from Harry Pitcher, shore captain for Secunda Marine, with orders to report to Halifax as soon as possible to undertake a tow job in the Gulf of St. Lawrence. The mission: to rescue the powerless vessel *Pal-Wind* and tow her to Sept-Îles, Quebec.

Clinton tells the story just as he would on a wharf on Grand Manan: "They called me at the house and asked me to get to Halifax as fast as I could. My wife and I got ready, and at 5:30 AM we arrived in Dartmouth. There must have been some speeding, as it is usually four-and-a-half hours drive. Anyway, we got there and it was raining, and snow, everything together. And the ship had just come out of dry dock and they were trying to get everything ready, trying to get bridles for towing on, and everything else ready to go. We departed by probably 6:30 AM, to head to the Gulf of St. Lawrence to pick up that ship. We had a good breeze going down along the shore, probably thirty-five or forty knots. We stopped at the locks at Cape Canso and picked up fuel there. By the time we went out through the locks and into the Gulf on Sunday, it was a perfect day. They were predicting easterly winds for that night, so we got across in the afternoon.

"That little ship was out of Peru. She had gone across the Atlantic, and unloaded cargo over there, and while they were there they picked up a couple of stowaways they didn't know they had aboard. When they got off Newfoundland, they lost all their engine power. They were there pretty near a week waiting for us to get there. They didn't have any stove, no fire, no heat. They had a crew of twenty-nine, the captain's wife was with them, and the two stowaways. We went alongside and the cook had made a couple of roast beef to give them. The coast guard had been out and asked to take the wife off, but she wouldn't go. The captain had told the crew that any of them could go. Nobody left him, they all stayed. He was a lieutenant in the Peru navy. He came and took this ship on his first trip into the North Atlantic. From what he told me, it was his last trip into the North Atlantic. Everything went on the ship. They probably didn't have enough fuel. Didn't plan on the extra wind, the tide.

"We picked them up in the afternoon, and by two in the morning the wind had increased up to thirty knots, and the captain called us to ask us to slow down as his propellor was turning and he didn't want his gear box ruined. We slowed down till he secured his propellor. We never went back up to full speed, that would be about eight knots. We dropped down to seven or eight force, and we were getting up to forty-five-knot winds. The second mate came down and asked me about reducing speed, and I told him to reduce back to fifty percent. We towed that way till about 5:00 AM when the chief mate came down and asked us to slow down even more, so I dropped it to twenty-five percent. We hadn't more than slowed down when I parted off the tow cable. I have to take the blame for this. I think that mate slowed down too fast, and the tow cable dropped down and got caught on the bottom, and the wind was blowing that ship so fast that it passed us and parted off the tow cable. He was adrift again. We chased him all that day. We chased him all over the Gulf of St. Lawrence with the wind blowing. We put a new tow cable up Monday afternoon, and that parted off again. I called the ship and told him when they got the tow cable back to put the shackle on over the wire, and instead of doing that, they put the rope around the wire and then put the shackle on over the rope, and that just chafed off. By that time the *Louis St. Laurent* had arrived on the scene. All the time we were chasing her up and down the St. Lawrence, my crew had to be on deck making up new tow cables, getting up wires, getting up ropes, so you had to decide whether to go with the ship the way she was going, or go your own way, and once the *Louis St. Laurent* arrived we repaired our tow cables and left them to watch the ship.

"Eventually, we got to the *Pal-Wind* again. At that time I put a rope out for them, and she parted off the rope, so we let her drift again for the next day, and the next day. We had food and fuel to last us two to three weeks. Tuesday night they called to say they were drifting ashore. I told him we'd try to get a rope out. By this time the wind was running eighty-five knots, and the sea was going fifty feet high and there was blinding snow. I was trying to get the ship into position and figure out how fast he was drifting. I wanted him to back his anchor off to the first shackle and shackle the anchor, and I would try to get in close enough to him so he could get his anchor chain out through the bow of the ship and on board the tug. We tried it, and it wasn't good, but we knew we had to get a line on him somehow. We shot these over with a rocket gun. I don't know how many times we went in and got blown back out.

"The chief engineer was in the wheelhouse with me. He'd been a deckhand who'd spent most of his time with me in the wheelhouse anyway; Dave Acalaca was his name. His father was Indian from Calcutta, and his mother was from Scotland. He was my engineer. He knew as much as the mates did. If the winch wasn't working, I brought Dave up. If the bow thruster wasn't working, I brought Dave up. When we were doing that job, he ran between me and the radar in the bow of the ship, and we'd lose her in the snow and he'd tell me where to find her. When he couldn't see her, I said, 'I can.' He asked where. I said, 'On the beach in the morning with all those people drowned. You keep looking for her.' When the Ocean Ranger went down I was there, and I saw all those bodies and I didn't want to see that again.

"They'd fire those rockets and they'd hit on our deck, and they'd come right up at me in the wheelhouse and every time you'd wonder if it was going to come right through that big window. Dave would hide behind me, and I'd try to move, and he'd say, 'Don't move, you damn fool, if it don't hit you, it's going to hit me.' They fired six rockets, we fired one, and the line wasn't made fast to the rocket. I don't know how far that thing went; last I saw, it was still going! The last line got both of us. We sent them a piece of eight-inch rope, they hauled that up between us and the *Pal-Wind*, made it fast on their anchor chain, and we winched it back aboard just like playing a big salmon on a trout line. If you parted off that piece of rope, goodbye, and you lost the anchor chain off that. They couldn't get it back on board as they had no power, so we had to make sure that we didn't break that eight-inch poly-prop rope off. The chain came out through and it didn't lead fair with the lead on the winch, so we'd haul it off, and they'd have to stop, lift it up and put it back on. Then we'd haul out some more, then they'd holler 'stop.' This was all radio communication with their captain, and he'd talk to his mate on the bow in Spanish.

"We finally got that chain down aboard and down on the deck of the supply ship. We had what was called cam-forks, round, came up out of the deck and had a top on it which was controlled by hydraulic power so you could put that chain on it and it clamped on the chain and held it. Once we had that aboard all we had to do was get our tow winch out on it. Then we had the ship. The wind was still blowing eighty-five knots. Our cook was in his sixties and he had food for that crew all the time. Once we finally had her we intended to tow to Sept-Îles in Quebec; that is where it was bound for. After I got the vessel, the radio operator in Stephenville came on and said that Search and Rescue in Halifax wanted to tell me where I could tow the vessel to, and I told her that she didn't want to hear me and Halifax didn't want to hear me, as I had been out there for a week with my crew bounding around, they've been sitting in a nice chair, going home every night. They wanted me to tow it to Sydney, and I told them I wasn't going to tow it to Sydney; it is going to Sept-Îles. She then told me they were commanding me to take it to Sydney, and I told her to get me my office on the phone, which she did. I talked to the shore captain, and he agreed that I was hired to take it to Sept-Îles, and that is where I was to go."

And that is where he did go.

Clinton has but one regret about the incident. "We got recognition from the province of Nova Scotia and we were identified as Nova Scotia seafarers. Well, this seafarer is proud to say he's a Grand Mananer through and through, and they should have said so," he said emphatically.

Retirement has not been easy for Clinton, who says, "I do miss the sea, I planned on working till seventy, made it to sixty-three and left for health reasons. I don't go down to the Saint John docks, as they won't let me in. Worked there since 1954 and they think I'm going to become a terrorist!" he laughs. He still enyoys going to his native island, especially the Ingalls Head area, "just to see if they do things as they did."

You can be certain he would follow the same career path today, and also sure that he would agree with the sailor in Charles Dibdin's poem when he turned to his buddy Billy and said,

We know what risks all landsmen run,
From noblemen to tailors
Then let us both thank Providence
That you and I are sailors.

Crystal Beach, Last of the Riverboat Beaches

When the last of the riverboats, the *D. J. Purdy,* stopped servicing the lower St. John River in 1947, many Saint John area picnickers lost the only way they had to reach upriver beaches such as Day's Landing, Carter's Point, Woodman's Point, and Oak Point. These were places where the government had built wharves so that goods from the city could be dropped off, produce from the country could be picked up, and passengers could conveniently disembark. And thousands did just that.

David and Dorothy Murchison, the operators of Crystal Beach.

Those who recollect such days say they were among the best of times, but when the riverboats ceased operating, city folk had to turn to city beaches such as Dominion Park on the river, Mispec Park on the Bay of Fundy, and Lily Lake in city-centre Rockwood Park for their summer beach experience. All of these had bus services, and offered essentially the same experience as the upriver beaches, except, of course, for the riverboat ride.

Without users, the privately held upriver beaches fell on hard times. Portions of some were sold off to various cottage owners who had cars and were eager to have a private place to enjoy summer. Other properties were kept open and operating, but with insufficient revenue to pay expenses, eventually many were taken by the government to pay back taxes. But such a sad fate has not befallen Crystal Beach, which since 1955 has been operated by David and Dorothy Murchison. Though it has been hard work, it has also brought them much joy and satisfaction.

David has connections with the beach that go back to his youth, when he spent the summers in what he called a "shanty that mom and dad rented from the Gorhams downriver from Crystal Beach." At that time, he explained, "Mr. and Mrs. Isaac Palmer owned the point of land, and it was a working farm. A concrete wharf had been built in 1929 to better serve the riverboats, and was known as Day's Landing. The Palmers allowed church groups that came by riverboat to hold their picnics at the beach. They had built a big barnboard pavilion at the shore, with a working kitchen and a wood stove where they could cook up hot dogs and corn on the cob. I stood in every food line," he laughed. "I was a Baptist one week, then an Anglican, United the next week. God gave me fast feet and I won a lot of the races they held."

Bustling church service at Crystal Beach.

In the early forties David's dad bought the property from the Palmers, intending to have his brother work it. In the mid-forties the riverboat service ended on the river and there was a quiet period before the motor vehicle age began in earnest. David recalled that time, saying, "When I was a young fella, Herb Day rented a few cottages in the area, but only Mr. Scott and Mrs. Porter had cars. People who rented the cottages would wait for either of them to head into town and hitch a ride."

He added, "Ralph Dick had operated the beach from the time the river-boats went off until I bought it. It was offered to my father first, but Pop didn't want anything to do with it. He lived next to the beach at the Palmer property so I knew the area intimately and I could see its possibilities, but if Art Gorman hadn't talked me into it, I wouldn't have bought it."

David had married only a year before buying the beach and credits his wife Dorothy (née Dykeman) with having had the "special talents that helped us develop the property and keep it going." By way of explanation, he said, "Dorothy was a farm girl from Jemseg and had worked in her grandfather's general store. She had just finished nursing training in Saint John, and this combination of experience proved to be just what we needed to run the beach, because you've got to love the river and know how to deal with people."

Dorothy recalled the first summer they operated Crystal. "When we moved into the old pavilion it seemed like it was about a hundred years old. It was twisted and dried out so badly there were huge gaps between the boards. It looked impossible to do anything with. At night we had to turn out the lights in our bedroom before we undressed, or everyone in the campsites would see a show," she laughed.

"Still," she continued, "I loved it right from the first day. I could lay out on the beach, talk with the girls, work on my tan. If someone wanted something, they would come and tap me on the shoulder and I would go in to get what they wanted."

David has a slightly different recollection of those days. "She is simplifying it," he says, explaining that in reality Dorothy was in the canteen seven days a week, working sixteen hours a day from the beginning. "That's a pattern she kept up till very recently," he noted.

Soon after they began their association with Crystal Beach, they had a Saint John visitor with some advice. Dorothy explained. "Seaward McDonald from the Tourist Department came to the site and told us, 'Camping is going to be big, and we had better get ready for it.'" At the time, a few tenters were showing up, but David and Dorothy had no facilities.

As Dorothy put it, "All we had was a pump for water, and everyone came to use it—the campers, the farmers, the cottagers. We had no bathrooms at all. When they closed the Jemseg schools, I sent David up to get the outhouses. I can still see the old truck coming across the field with them bouncing on the back of the truck."

David laughed at this memory, and added: "We started charging the campers fifty cents a night to pitch a tent right on the beach. Sometimes there would be so many of them on the beach that we couldn't see the river from the canteen. Their demands grew and grew. They had water and bathrooms, but then they wanted power. Trailers came and wanted power, water, and sewerage right to the trailers. There was a huge swamp out in back of the pavilion and alders grew right up to the back door. We could only accommodate twelve cars the first couple of years, but that was enough because most people still didn't have cars and came to Westfield by bus or train, and walked up to the beach."

Improvements to the site were done as money permitted. "We were offered government help, but we did it on our own," Dorothy noted. "Too independent to do anything else," David added. One of the first big improvements was putting in a jukebox and opening up the pavilion for dancing. The kids soon discovered that they could listen to music all day long if they just put in a single nickel and then kicked the machine, but their days of cheap dancing were short-lived. As Dorothy explained with a chuckle, "One day [the jukebox] caught fire. I was in the canteen, and I ran in to see what was wrong. When I saw what was happening I got a bucket of water and threw it on the jukebox. That was the end of the jukebox."

That setback did not stop the improvements. Once the land behind the canteen was filled in, an adjacent field was developed so that forty trailers could be accommodated and there was room for fifteen tent sites. Nine quaint cabins were also built for the cottagers to enjoy, and more pavilion improvements were done, including the construction of a rustic pub with paintings of historic river scenes on its exterior.

When the 1929 wharf became available, it was bought. Of that, David said, "We had little choice. The wharves were going to be sold, and they were all in bad shape. They were built in the Depression era as make-work projects, and they are falling in on themselves. We've patched ours up, but in its present state, cars are not allowed on the wharf and no boats are welcome to tie up alongside of the wharf. Such as it is, it is for our guests to enjoy."

Though David and Dorothy originally thought the beach property might produce sufficient income on which to raise a family, it soon became obvious that this was not the case. David remained at his job at Saint John Shipbuilding, and later began working as a longshoreman on the docks of Saint John, an occupation that allowed him to have most days free in the summer to devote to the development of the beach. "The jobs seem quite opposite in nature," David notes, "but I loved both. After a summer of dealing with the public twenty-four hours a day, seven days a week, it was nice to go back to the docks where you hardly had to speak to a soul." Technically, David is retired from his day job, but in reality he has just assumed more and more roles at the beach, and his dream of improving the property seems never-ending.

Both David and Dorothy admit that the public can be demanding, yet both also declare that the people they have met over fifty years of running Crystal Beach have made it all worthwhile. In Dorothy's words, "Every year there is some child who becomes special to you, is really the pet of the beach. Maybe you only know them for a season and never see them for years, then one day, fully grown, perhaps hiding behind a beard, or with long locks of hair, they show up and say hello."

Dorothy and David are hopeful that their son Mark and his sister Leah will one day take over the operation of the Crystal Beach attraction. Asked what he thought of that, Mark said, "I'd always assumed that, but you'll have to ask Dad and Mom if they think it might happen. The beach has always been part of my summer. It is a lot of work, but I love it. I'm trying to get them to retire, but they don't seem ready to go yet," he laughed.

If Mark and Leah do take over, it would ensure that the last riverboat vacationland will live on. "I'd like that," Dorothy said, "It's scary to think of not being here, but it's nice to think that what we worked so hard to build will endure."

Fredericton's Town Clock Keeps On Ticking

Wayne Stewart is responsible for the maintenance of more than a hundred buildings owned by the City of Fredericton, but his favourite is definitely City Hall, and its tower clock.

"When I took on this job in 1997, there was very little information about the clock, and how to look after it," he said as he led me up the series of stairs and attic walkways leading to the cupola and the clock.

He explained that Fredericton's City Hall had burnt down in 1875, and Mayor Edward L. Wetmore and council decided to rebuild on the same spot. "The plan was to have a 115-foot tower to accommodate a bell for fire alarm purposes," Wayne noted, adding, "During construction the plan was modified to add the clock with its eight-foot dials seventy-five feet over street level."

Wayne Stewart and an up-close view of the machinery behind Fredericton's City Hall Clock.

When Wetmore left office, the clock still wasn't in place. The next mayor, George E. Fenety, offered his yearly salary of two hundred dollars toward the completion of the project, and several other city officials then came forward to contribute. James White was given forty dollars to go to Boston to study tower clocks in that city and make a recommendation.

Wayne explained that the mechanism selected on White's recommendation is by Gillette and Bland of Croydon Clock Works in London, England. He added, "It was done at a cost of $1,748.83 and the installation was supervised by Sir Edmund Beckett, an official of the Greenwich Observatory." With the bell, which was bought in Boston at the William Blake Foundry, the total cost was $2,320.62

The average person can't visit the tower, as it requires negotiating some very narrow stairways, a lot of ducking under and crawling over beams, and walking some bouncy planking high over the council chamber and city offices. "You're lucky to be able to get in here, Dave," he told me on the day I was able to visit. "Not everyone is as steady on their feet as you are," he added with a chuckle.

For those who have not had the up-close look I was able to get, Wayne is working on a brochure that will show photos of the works, the bell, and the faces of the clock, which is wound three times a week.

"It's the oldest mechanically operated clock in the oldest continuously used city hall in the province," he explained.

In all its years of use, the clock has witnessed major changes in the science of timekeeping. As Wayne explained, Fredericton once had three official times. "There was Eastern Standard used by the railway, Atlantic Standard by the post office, and sun time used by the Cathedral." These days, everyone uses the same time—but daylight saving time causes some minor complication. In the fall of each year, Wayne has to stop the clockworks for an hour to change to standard time. "It's easier in the spring," he noted, "as it just has to be moved ahead an hour."

He added, "Over the years there have been problems with the clock from time to time, but we've always been able to get parts and keep it going.... Sometimes the clock has stopped on its own. Ice would do it, and a couple of years back, computer wires blew into the driving rods and it stopped." He added with a laugh, "It was a case of new technology meeting old, and new won."

However, he noted, the problem was soon overcome, and the clock ticks on. With any luck at all, it should do so for decades to come.

Disaster at McIntosh Cove— New Brunswick's Worst Train Wreck

It was while cycling the abandoned rail line between Caraquet and Bathurst that I came across the story of the Caraquet train wreck, succinctly told on a plaque placed on the trestle bridge that spans the Caraquet River at McIntosh Cove. It seemed an innocent enough spot that June night a few years ago, and it must have seemed the same to conductor Daniel Kearney and engine driver Michael Lanagan when they came upon the cove on the afternoon of December 17, 1887.

It was the dead of winter, of course. The engine, with a Stackhouse snowplow on front and a tender and passenger car behind, had travelled from Caraquet, and though there was eighteen inches of snow in most places, the train had not experienced any problems. The track over the ice-edged river was bare, but there was a huge drift of snow on the western side of the trestle. It had to be dealt with so that the remaining thirty-five miles to Bathurst could be cleared and the line could be opened once again to regular traffic. It's hard to understand why this was considered to be so urgent when one reads accounts of the history of the line, such as that by David Nason in

Railways of New Brunswick, which notes that the Caraquet railway was never a money-maker.

But that December day it must have seemed important to cut through that big drift, and it must not have seemed an insurmountable task to those in charge of that train.

To discern the full story, I consulted several newspapers of the era, and while the tale is generally the same in each, small differences from one to another help to understand the tragedy more fully.

The best account was that of the *Saint John Daily Sun*, which appeared on Monday, December 19, 1887, the next publishing day after the accident. It was written by a correspondent in Bathurst and marked as "Special to the Sun." In the style of the time, that author is not given a byline. In part, the report read:

A thrill of horror ran through Bathurst yesterday evening, when it was learned that a terrible accident had occurred on the Caraquet railway, by which many lives were lost. It was at first reported that a train had crashed

The McIntosh Cove steam engine accident can be effectively told at Hopewell Cape, where this old steamer is on display.

through Caraquet bridge, and that 10 persons had been killed, but a little later particulars arrived showing that the bridge had not given away, and that the loss of life had been confined to eight, though five others were severely injured.

The account asserts that the engineer, Mr. Lanagan, "at once whistled down brakes, reversed his engine, and brought the train to a standstill." It then goes on to explain how the accident happened:

The snow plow, engine and tender were then detached from the balance of the train, which was left standing on the track, the intention being to run back for them as soon as the drift had been pierced by the snow plow. Prompted by a curiosity that led to his death, Frank Miller, one of the passengers, got on board of the engine with driver Lanagan and conductor Kearney, to see how the plow would strike the drift and what the result would be. The other passengers remained in the [detached passenger] car. There were a number of hands on the train who went along to assist in removing the snow and doing whatever other work might be necessary to clear the track. There was no snow on the bridge and nothing but a clear track between the spot where the train had been halted and the high drift on the other side of the structure. Under a good head of steam, the snow plow, engine and tender dashed forward, the driver's intention being to strike the obstruction with as much force as possible considering the short run, but when about half way across the bridge, the snow plow left the track and [was] followed by the engine and cab mounted [on] the guard rail, where they each seemed to hang an instant, and plunged into the river, a distance of about 15 feet, and hurtling eight men into eternity, and injuring five others.

All the papers of the day listed the victims of the tragic accident, including whatever information was available about each. The *Moncton Daily Times* of December 19 identified them as follows: .

Conductor Kearney of Douglastown, Miramichi, single, aged 25 years

Driver Lanergan [identified in other papers as Lanagan or Lanigan] Bathurst, married with four children, aged 31

Felix Boucher, fireman, Bathurst, single, aged 24

Joseph Vienneau, section man, Bathurst, married with 5 children, aged 30

John Paulin, section man, Caraquet, married, with large family, aged 30

Octave Pinet, section man, Caraquet, single, aged 23

John Carney, Bathurst, married with five children

Frank Miller, Bathurst, single, aged 20

The *Saint John Daily Sun* arranged an interview with the railway's superintendent of construction, P. H. Melvin of Bathurst, who was able to give a first-hand account from an expert's point of view. It was printed on December 20, 1887.

On Sunday morning, in company with Mann, I went to the scene of the accident. We found the upper part of a block moved somewhere in the vicinity of two feet, which made the rails about two feet out of position. The beds of the timbers were broken off, undoubtedly done by the engine on its downward course. The engine quite likely moved the rails some when it struck. This is the only damage to the bridge, and it is complete in every other respect. Not even a rail is missing. A block being out of place is undoubtedly due to the severe gale and storm on Friday night. During the height of this storm the tide was never known to be so high for a number of years. Scows up on the marsh for three years were never touched by water before, while they were swept away. The great pressure of ice at high tide forced the block out of position, the great gale blowing sending the ice against it, and from the heights of the wind, it must have pounded the bridge with tremendous force. On Sunday I saw James Lordon, and he said that he was sitting in the engine along with Con. Kearney and Frank Miller....[Lordon said that the driver, Lanigan], looking out of the cab window, cried out, "My God, the bridge is broken." Lanigan reversed the engine and he [Lordon] says he saw Lanigan's hand reach for the whistle and next Lordon remembered was some time after, when he found himself in a neighbor's house.

Lordon's face was cut and his pockets full of glass, left hand cut and both legs with scald marks on them, all of which proves that Lordon was shot through the cab window. Notwithstanding that, Lordon doesn't remember anything. He walked to a neighboring house. While at the scene of the accident I heard men say that a man waved his hand as a signal for the train to stop, but never having any idea what it meant, and being accustomed to people waving their hands and handkerchiefs at the trains, no attention was paid to it.

As would be expected, an inquest followed. It was held by Coroner Blackball at Caraquet on December 21. The *Miramichi Leader* report on this read, in part:

That Daniel Kearney, Felix Bouche, Michael Lanagan, John Carney, Joseph Viennot, Octave Pinette, Frank Miller and John Louis Paulin, came to their death on Saturday, 17th December inst. between the hours of two and three, standard time, in the afternoon by being precipitated with an engine and tender, while on a bridge of the Caraquet railway in the Parish of Caraquet, known as the Mackintosh Cove bridge, into the river, said engine and tender being, at the time, in charge of the employees of the Caraquet Railway Company.

After examination of the bodies the jury find that Michael Lanagan was crushed under the engine, and that John Carney was killed by a log falling over him from the bridge while he was holding on to the tender after it had fallen in the river; and that the other men were drowned or crushed.

We attribute the cause of the disaster to the derangement of a portion of the above named bridge, caused by the action of ice against said bridge during a storm, and the unusual high tide of the day previous, the sixteenth of December, instant.

As to how far the Superintendent of the road, who had charge of the train that day, is responsible for taking the track-men from the section of the road where the accident occurred, we are not prepared to say, as by the evidence of two of the employees of the road, and by his own evidence, "the Superintendent gave orders to the engine driver not to cross the bridge before it was examined."

It is the opinion of the jury that the said railway bridge was defective in its plan in that it had no protection from side pressure, such as from ice during a high tide, and we censure the Government inspectors for accepting such a railway bridge, situated, as it is, in a tide way.

The jury exonerated the trackmen of the section of the railway where the accident occurred, as they had been taken off that section to do duty elsewhere by the orders of the superintendent, and had not an opportunity to examine the bridge before the engine passed over it.

Although the Caraquet railway line made money in only two of its first twenty years of operation (1874–1894) and suffered through a number of other tragedies and mishaps after this initial period, portions of it remained in operation until 1992, under various owners and different names. Since then it has been abandoned, and the track bed now serves hikers and cyclists. Today, the marker at McIntosh Cove is the only visible reminder of the most disastrous incident in the railway's long history.

Scouting Takes Off in New Brunswick

The Scouting movement has become such a common feature of childhood that it's hard to imagine a time when it didn't exist. It's worth remembering that the movement is only a hundred years old, having begun in 1907 in England and just three years later in New Brunswick, when the founder, Lord Baden Powell, came to Saint John to begin the work.

The first mention of the new movement in New Brunswick was in an article titled "Baden Powell Coming," which appeared in the *Saint John Globe* on Tuesday, July 5, 1910. Then, on September 12, 1910, the paper reported,

General Sir Robert Baden Powell took Saint John by surprise when he descended unheralded on the city Sunday and looked around for a cab. He soon met the president and officers of the Canadian Club, the president and secretary of the exhibition association, and had arranged to hold a public meeting in the interests of the Boy Scout movement, and to review a patrol of Boy Scouts.... The Opera House was well filled this afternoon for the talk on the Boy Scouts movement delivered by General Baden Powell. Mr. Miles E. Agar, president of the Canadian Club presided. His worship the Mayor, and members of the common council and others occupied seats on the platform.... As he stepped on the platform and as he explained the formation and discipline of the Boy Scouts he was frequently interrupted by hearty applause.

On Monday, September 19, 1910, the headlines announced, "Boy Scout movement organized on Saturday. Committee appointed to name a provincial council." By Saturday, September 24, 1910, Scouts had been organized on the West Side. The Globe reported:

At an enthusiastic meeting of twenty-five boys held in the schoolroom of St. Judes Church, in West Saint John on Friday evening a troop of Scouts was organized. Three patrols were formed, a fourth will shortly be com-

A typical scene of a scouting camp in Sussex.

pleted. Rev. G. F. Scovil is to be the Scoutmaster and the assistant is Mr. Joseph Smith who has had wide experience in the Boy's Brigade work, and in the militia. The boys elected as patrol leaders Barry Smith, Merlyn Harding and Harold Cunningham for patrols number one, two and three, and Gordon McLeod for leader of number four when organized. As soon as the provincial association is organized a report will be made asking for authorization of the steps that have been taken and a confirmation of the appointments. In the meantime the boys are going ahead with their work. Some of the preliminary instructions were taken up last evening and this afternoon the troop will take a trip to the woods for the purpose of securing practical knowledge.

This was the first Boy Scout troop in the province, though later it was designated the 5th St. Jude's. For reasons that are not clear, the uptown Saint John troops got numbers one through four, suggesting that they were formed earlier, though there is no proof that they were.

Fredericton was next, and a headline in the *Daily Gleaner* of November 10, 1910, declared, "The Boy Scouts Movement Given a Start Here. Two patrols have been formed among the Church of England boys of the city. Others expected to organize soon. Officers elected and the boys have already had their first field work." The text of the article provided more information:

The first two patrols of the Boy Scouts have been formed in Fredericton and the members are boys of the Church of England congregations. It is anticipated that the boys of other churches will quickly organize and in a short time there will be a large Fredericton troop. There are 17 boys in the first two patrols and it is expected that another patrol will be organized in the course of a few days.... The Very Rev. Dean Schofield, assisted by Sargent Ryder, RCR, had conducted examinations necessary before any applicant can become a member. The patrols are formed under the Baden Powell Boy Scouts plan and the members sworn in are then known as tenderfeet. The officers of the two patrols are Patrol Leader Stirling Brannen

Jr., [Unclear] Boone, and Corporals Ralph McKenzie and Joe Oldham. Already the members of the new patrols have had their first tramp in the county, and in a few days will have their first practice at trapping and other work to be taken up.

Just a few days after Fredericton's successful start in Scouting, it was reported in the November 14 *Moncton Daily Times* that there would be Boy Scouts for Moncton and that the Daughters of the Empire were to undertake the work of the organization. Just four days later, on November 18, the *Daily Times* noted,

The meeting of young boys that was held last evening in the 19th Battery Headquarters for the purpose of forming Boy Scouts was a grand success. Between 60 and 70 members were enrolled after which instructive lessons were given by Major Anderson and Captain W. A. McKee. Both these gentlemen pointed out the object of the organization.... Uniforms, instruction, books, etc., will be taken up at the next meeting. It is hoped that all the young fellows will come forward and enlist so that Moncton can boast of having the leading Boy Scout organization in the Maritimes Provinces.

Official sanction came later, when on January 27, 1911, the *Moncton Daily Times* reported on the establishment of the Boy Scout Association by four churches, Central Methodist, St. George's, Highfield Street Baptist, and an unnamed Presbyterian church, all of which had Scout troops. It was pointed out that before the association could carry on its work, its charter had to be obtained from the national scouting headquarters in Ottawa, and a Mr. Coulthurst was instructed to communicate with the proper authorities in Ottawa.

Thus did Scouting get its start in New Brunswick. It has had a grand run, which is now approaching a century. Like thousands of other New Brunswick boys, I was a Scout and I can certainly say that I benefited from the movement that Lord Baden Powell was able to spread around the globe.

Public Schools and Pulp Mills: Chatting with Travis Cushing

Travis Cushing always has a story (or two...or three...) for me anytime I find time to visit him in his Quinton Heights home in Saint John West. Struggling with partial loss of hearing, and full loss of his eyesight, he says sharing stories is one of the only old-time delights he can still pursue in his ninth decade. He's always glad to have an audience. I shared some of his stories in my book *West Side Stories*, but he's got plenty more. On a recent visit, he shared stories about his work as a teacher and a school administrator from the forties to the eighties. He then

Travis Cushing holds a clipping that brings to mind a story...

went way back to the turn of the twentieth century for some tales his father had shared about the mill the Cushing Family owned at the Reversing Falls. The family lived next to the mill, which stood on an island across a canal at what was called Union Point. Today the canal is long gone and the site is occupied by the Irving pulp mill.

Travis began with some interesting stories about the old school board office at the corner of Union and Hazen avenues, which is now a Vito's Restaurant: "The school board office was for many years located in a former distillery and one-time cigar factory. Dr. W. H. McKenzie, a former superintendent of schools in Saint John, turned up this interesting bit of history some years ago, and subsequent investigation discovered the remains of the foundations of the stills in the basement of the building. The building was used as a distillery, and later as a cigar factory; the retail business occupied the first floor, and the proprietors and their families lived on the upper floors, reached by a graceful staircase rising from the entrance hall. When the school board acquired the building, the upper floors were converted to classrooms and the overflowing classes of grade nine boys that had been housed previously in the old synagogue, situated near the present parking lot, were moved in. During World War II these classrooms were again converted to house the training programs for radio operators and technicians, and hundreds of these students graduated from that building. So great was the demand for radio operators that for a time the facilities were operated twenty-four hours a day."

Many firsts occurred when the board was in this building. "The Board of School Trustees of Saint John was the first board in New Brunswick to computerize its payroll and accounting procedures. It was overseen by Mr. Frank Christiansen, secretary of the board for many years, and Gerald S. Brewer, then assistant superintendent (business)," Travis explained. "It was not, however, without some problems that almost seemed divinely driven," he said with a chuckle.

He explained, "At one point early in the use of the computer, it produced paycheques for the teaching sisters that were fourteen dollars larger than the cheques for the lay teachers. A service man was called in to correct the problem, but in no time at all, the computer was again favouring the sisters. This time the manufacturer of the equipment claimed the problem arose from voltage fluctuations, and we had a new electrical entrance installed. Still the computer erred. Finally we changed to a new computer and the problem was solved."

The voltage fluctuations, Travis noted, were due to the close proximity to the mid-city power plant that stood just a block west on Union Street, below Dock. "At least, that is what we were told by the computer experts, but there were a lot of people who thought there was a higher power behind those higher paycheques," he chuckled.

Travis also had some interesting stories about the history of other school buildings. In 1967, School District #20 lost several schoolhouses at the time of the amalgamation of seventeen districts into one as part of the Robichaud-led Equal Opportunity Program, which reduced the number of school districts in New Brunswick from several hundred to thirty-three. This created a problem with surplus properties that were left standing empty all over the province. Many were converted to cottages or homes, or became community halls. That was the case with the schoolhouse at Little Lepreau, but it took a more roundabout route along the way.

"In the amalgamation process, the one-room school at Little Lepreau, like a number of others, became surplus, as pupils were accommodated in larger schools and bussed there," Travis recalled. "To protect the abandoned school against vandalism, the maintenance staff of the new district shuttered windows and padlocked doors. One day, on a routine check, a board maintenance man discovered that the padlock on the Little Lepreau school had been changed and he could not get in. Inquiry at the neighborhood store revealed that a local couple, newly married, required a site for their reception and had used the school, after breaking the padlock. This did not, of course, please the board at all, and at a meeting with the couple, it was suggested that it would have been more appropriate to have asked permission of the school board. However, they informed the baord that they had received permission from Miss Ruth Hanson. It happened that Miss Hanson was a teacher in the district and a telephone call to her soon cleared the matter up.

"You see," Travis continued, "Miss Hanson explained that her grandfather, who was a resident of Little Lepreau, had built the school about 1890 with a view to encouraging education in the area, and had loaned it, together with the land on which it was located, to the school board for use as a school, as long as it was needed, but it was to revert to his estate and heirs when it was no longer required.

So Miss Hanson simply said she had repossessed the building and made it available for community purposes."

And it served as such for many years thereafter.

Having spent decades in the school system, Travis has lots of stories about student discipline and the comical situations that sometimes result from it. He still gets a chuckle from one story involving a teacher who conscientiously asked every tardy student for an explanation: "One morning the city was in the grip of a blizzard so severe that many pupils did not get to school at all. One young man, who made a valiant effort, finally struggled in twenty minutes late, and was immediately accosted by the conscientious teacher for an excuse as to his tardiness. The snow-covered student paused barely a moment before responding, with tongue in cheek, 'Sorry, Sir, I am late because my lead dog froze to a fire hydrant.'" No more questions were asked, then or in the future.

Travis also chuckles at another story of a student with a snappy comeback. "Some pupils are not only intelligent, but also very quick witted," he noted. "One such pupil in a grade ten high school class had been so restless and annoying that finally his teacher, a young man, ordered him from the classroom for the rest of the period. The boy dawdled and delayed, opening and closing his desk, rearranging his books, until the teacher could tolerate no more. He seized the boy by the seat of his pants and the collar of his jacket and rushed him toward the door which was closed. At the last moment the boy exclaimed: 'Not the key hole! Please, sir, not the keyhole!'"

Of course, such discipline would be considered unacceptable today, but you can be sure that students and teachers are still getting into amusing clashes, and we should hope that someone like Travis is there to record them for posterity.

Taking a step back in time from his teaching stories, Travis shared some amusing anecdotes of life at the old Cushing mill.

How Travis's father shocked Travis's mother: "I didn't hear this story till I was an adult and a Mr. McIntyre at the Turnbull Home asked me if I had ever heard about the time my father had shaved off his beard. I had to say that he hadn't told me. It seems that Mother, when they were newly wed, had nagged him about the fact that he wore a beard and other young men his age didn't wear beards. So one Saturday night while on his way home from work at the sawmill, he had stopped and had his beard shaved off. He came in quite late, and went to the dressing room off the master bedroom, and prepared for bed. As he climbed into the bed, Mother woke up and saw this strange man with a pale face in her room. She screamed bloody murder, and Mr. McIntyre, the storyteller in this case, who happened to be a stable boy back then, rushed out across the street to see what the problem was. To his surprise, it was my father, who Mother had thought to be a pale-faced intruder in her bedroom. Father was not long growing his beard back, Mr. McIntyre told me."

How a tramp almost drowned in the canal by the mill: "The family lived right beside the canal down by the sawmill, and tramps used to come to the door, and Mother had been instructed to turn them away. This one tramp didn't leave soon enough to suit the dog, who chased him, and the man ran and fell into the canal. The dog, being a Newfoundland dog, wouldn't let him drown. So the dog jumped in to rescue the man. The poor tramp thought that the dog was going to kill him. Fortunately, Mother came to get the dog, and the man escaped."

Byron and the donkey named Jesus: "Dad was having the family for dinner on a Sunday and had invited the pastor of their church to join them. Their dining room overlooked the back lawn, which ran down to the river. Sometimes, donkeys used in the mill would grub for grass, but this was not a permitted feeding area, as mother wanted some grass around the house. Knowing this, my older brother Byron interrupted the dinnertime conversation to say, 'Jesus is on the back lawn.' Of course, this was quite a shock to all to hear, and Mother wanted to know what he meant. He pointed out the donkeys and said the one nearest the house was named 'Jesus' and that he was one of the donkeys at the mill. When queried on the name,

Byron said he'd never heard it called anything but 'Jesus' by the men trying to get it to do its work."

Travis's father's archaeological discovery: "I remember Dad bringing a saw home, he said that if I didn't believe there had been some early settlers in the area, he would prove it. He showed me a cannonball that had been embedded in a tree they were sawing, and which, when cut, took the teeth off the saw."

As our get-together was coming to an end, Travis filled me in on the history of the family mill. About 1900, he explained, "The supply of saw logs was getting difficult, the big trees were simply all cut near Saint John, and the Cushings thought that they could switch to pulp and make more money. And so Uncle George and Dad—Uncle George was the mover—found a partner named Partington, from England, who would put up money for a pulp mill. They built the first mill, and the market for pulp went bad and they didn't make enough money to pay off the loan, so they went bankrupt around 1905. There were at least two more owners before the Irvings bought it in 1945."

The Cushing mill, however, was the money behind Travis's education. He explained, "Dad died when I was fifteen, just before I went to university. Two relatives in the USA came up with fifty dollars each a month to put me through university. They were my brother Byron, known to all his friends in the states as George, and my paternal uncle Will, who was Will Channing Cushing, and they paid my tuition. My uncle Will received an honorary degree at UNB. He received that for developing the railway right-of-way between Chicago and St. Louis. He was the chief engineer for the Pennsylvania Railway. He gave a paper in France on developing right-of-way, and he worked his entire life for the Pennsylvania Railway. I later got into the education field, and UNB gave me an honorary degree for 'distinguished service' to the education field in New Brunswick. Mine was in about 1946, and Will's was in 1915."

Quite a distinction for one family to get two honorary degrees!

Maebelle and Bernardine: Two Gals, Two Hundred Years of Life, and Still Loving It

Sometimes writing isn't all it's cracked up to be. It can be tiring, tedious, and solitary work. After much research, it requires hours and hours of staring at a little blue screen, typing and retyping letters, arranging and rearranging words, checking and rechecking facts, puzzling over punctuation, fighting over sentence structure, and arguing, mostly with myself, over what to include, what to leave out. Most days, it is a slow process, and the muscles in the rear end and behind the shoulder blade and in the wrists begin to protest. Sometimes it is just not possible to listen to the message these muscles are trying to send: "Get up! Get out!" Some days, there is a deadline looming and one just has to plod on, taking satisfaction that one more page is done and the project is that much nearer to completion. Because when it's done, I can get back to the part I enjoy the most.

Bernardine Bohan and Frances Cullen at Bernardine's one hundredth birthday celebration.

And that part is meeting the people who share their stories— people like Maebelle Mellenger and Bernardine Bohan, whom I interviewed in 2005 when they were both celebrating their hundredth birthdays. You don't get to do many such interviews. In fact, in doing some three thousand stories over the past thirty years, these were the first two people I had met who had passed the century mark. Neither of them had any idea why they had been spared so long, but, as both of them were still active in various ways, I concluded that the secret might be good genes, combined with their passion for life. I asked both of them to share a few memories of their earliest years and both had solid stories—in fact, many more than I could relate here.

Maebelle's were of learning to drive in Saint John, and attending the first-ever Girl Guide camp on Long Island, in the Kennebecasis River, just north of the city in which she was born. And this is what she said: "I was about twelve when I first tried to drive. It was in the sheds where the Boston Boat came in at Reed's Point in the South End of Saint John. My dad was A. C. Currie, the manager of Eastern Steamships, and one day, as he was busy with arrivals or paperwork at the office, my friend Carlene Schmidt and I took Father's Saxon and drove it around the shed. As Carlene shouted out the commands '1-2-3 honk,' I shifted and blew the horn as directed. In no time, I got the hang of it, and as the shed door was open, we went out and up Water Street to the foot of King. There we saw a policeman and just then the car stalled. The policeman came over and cranked the machine and got us going again. We drove up Prince William Street and returned to the Reed's Point shed. As I thought the policeman might tell dad what we were up to, we confessed, and he decided as we were going to drive, we might as well learn to do it properly, and Dad proceeded to give lessons."

That skill paid off, as she and her husband Rex Mellenger visited twenty-two countries around the globe during their long marriage, travelling mostly by van before it was the stylish thing to do. She continued driving until she was almost a hundred years old, and was known to pick up her "old" friends (all younger than her) for grocery shopping.

Another early memory is of having been a founding member of the 1st Saint John Trinity Girl Guide Company, and attending the first Girl Guide camp ever held in New Brunswick, on Long Island in 1920. "At least I think we were on Long Island," she said. "Perhaps you better just say we were on an island in the Kennebecasis—I am sure of that," she laughed.

She has a collection of photos from the camp that help to keep her memory of the event fresh. Even though there is no one alive who might dispute the fact, Mrs. Mellenger would not comment on anything she did not recall personally. For example, she has no idea how they got from uptown Saint John's Trinity Church to the Kennebecasis, or how they got out to the island itself. Fortunately, the pictures, though faded, speak for themselves. One shows all twenty-three girls lined up with the notation, "Well, boys, here we are!" In the background is a big bell tent. "I imagine we borrowed them from the Scouts, but I can't say that for sure," Maebelle said. Another photo shows the girls all in a line with the cut under the picture describing the scene as "The snoozin' Quarters," in reference to the tents they used as shelter. "We didn't sleep, though, as much as you would imagine, and that is the reason for the question mark you see under that photo," she laughed.

Maebelle can't quite recall if they swam at the camp, but she says, "We must have, as there's a sort of a memory there. I just don't recall any change of clothing especially for swimming, so it might have been quite informal, perhaps only wading to cool off." In reference to swimming and general camp programs, Maebelle said, "Things were quite relaxed, you know. There weren't a lot of rules like you have now, [nor] a lot of regimentation or program. We were there, we enjoyed the time away from the city."

Throughout her life, Maebelle continued the friendship with Carlene Schmit, which began with the wild auto ride and was augmented by the Girl Guide experience, with membership in Trinity Sunday school, sea trips to Boston, and other events. "She could always make me laugh," Mabelle said. And perhaps that was the secret to her long life.

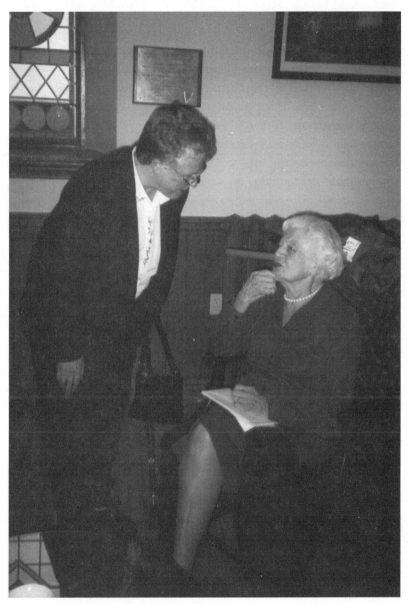

Joan Neill (left) talks with Maebelle Mellenger (right).

I was able to be with her in January of 2005 when she marked her hundredth birthday at Trinity Church, where she still reads the lessons. And then in late September, I was in the Lions Hall in Bath to watch Bernardine Bohan enter her hundredth birthday party, where she left her walker by her side long enough to do a little jig, to show off her agility and pay homage to her Irish roots, of which she is so proud.

It had been a little over five years since Bernardine Bohan had contacted me to tell me she found the "Local Lore" columns I was doing for the *Telegraph Journal* "very interesting and down to earth" and suggested she "might have a story or two to share." With that in mind, I paid her a visit, and among other things, she told me she would be one hundred years old on September 25, 2005, and that I would be invited to her party, as "I want some good-looking men around me that day." It was an invitation I could not refuse.

Over the years we had met, talked on the phone, exchanged letters, and I had learned a lot about the life of Bernardine. She often said to me, "I hope I reach a hundred, and if I do, I hope I know who I am." She certainly did, and she also knew everyone else gathered there that day.

I wasn't privy to all the conversations she had that day, but I bet she shared some of the same stories she'd told me over the years. Perhaps the one about when her family were the leading merchants of Bath. Their store sold groceries, clothing, shoes, millinery, and served as the post office. When she was just a wisp of a girl, it was an exciting place to be. Once, when she was given the job of watching the customers, she noted a very elegant lady picking over the combs, which were very fashionable at the time. She noted she dropped one of the combs into her muff, while she took another to the clerk to purchase it. Bernardine challenged her, saying, "Do you want to buy the one in the muff too?"

She clearly recalls her grandfather's death in 1915: "He was eighty-three. I remember the preparations for the funeral. The wake was in the house in which I now live. [She was born in the big rambling house at the foot of Monquart Hill where the family mercantile business began, and she still lives there today.] The family was all dressed in black. Big hams were cooked on the wood stove. Friends came by horse and sleigh, and had to have a meal."

Among other memories of her early years were the Arbour Day celebrations at the school. "We planted trees and put fish in the hole to fertilize them," she recalled. "In winter, we skated on Galen Drost's Pond on skates screwed on our boots. One night, Mr. Larlee, who was a big man, came out to skate with his wife, a tiny little woman. He tripped and fell on top of her, and then he just swept her up in his arms and carried her off to safety. It's a picture I'll never forget," she laughed.

From the shopkeeping days she vividly recalled the stocks of bananas as a new feature of the time. "They came in big crates," she said, "and they were hung up on a big nail for sale. My father would let me eat all the grapes I wanted, but not the bananas, as they were too expensive." In that era, Bernardine recalled, "there was a lot of bartering done, especially of eggs and butter, which were shipped from Bath to Saint John by train and would arrive in the big city the day after they had been bartered in their store."

Many times when she told me these stories, she'd say with a laugh, "I smile when I hear people talking about the good old days. When I hear people today say, 'I've had a busy day,' I think, 'Well, they had no water to carry, no tub to fill for laundry, no iron to heat on the stove.' Still, they think they're busy."

Though now over a hundred, she still enjoys her days in the family home writing letters, quilting, knitting, and embroidering. Just recently, she put up some peach and raspberry jam, and made a batch of choke cherry wine to enjoy when guests call. And they do call with some regularity, and when they do, they hear story after story about the times long past.

Once when I arrived, I had the most amazing experience. It was a Sunday, November 14, 2002, and I was driving to Johnville for a visit with my friend Frances Cullen. I asked her to let Bernardine know I would make a stop at her Bath home about 3:00 PM. When I arrived, Bernardine greeted me warmly, and said, "I've been expecting you for a couple of days now and have dug out some material I know you'll be interested in." I let the "couple of days" remark pass, thinking she was probably confused with the phone call from Frances, but as I was to find out, she wasn't a bit mixed up.

She reached toward the table beside her easy chair, and was soon leafing though a tiny notebook with brittle yellowed pages as if she were looking for something that would be of interest to me. After a bit I said, "Bernardine, you are just about the oldest person I know, and I was wondering if you might have any childhood recollections about Santa Claus."

"Why do you think I got this book out?" she asked. She explained that it was her Aunt Kate's diary, and on the page she had opened, 1911, there was an account of a visit by her Aunt Kate playing the role of Santa Claus in the very room where we were sitting. "I can recall that incident as if it were yesterday," Bernardine said with a laugh. Then she added the clincher: "It took me a while to find this old diary, but I knew it was what you wanted to talk about two days ago, so I dug till I found it."

You could have knocked me over with Santa's fur cap that day, as I left convinced that she really did know I was coming to gather a Christmas story, even though it was only mid November.

She's surprised me many times since and I hope she will continue to do so for a long time to come. I also hope I will continue to hear her fond farewell when I take leave from my visits. Many women could not get away with it, but Bernardine can and does. As I am about to depart, she will get a big gleam in her eye and a broad smile on her face, as she says, "Let me have a good look at you David. You might be the last man I will ever see." That's Bernardine, a hundred years in the making and still full of life!